MW00943979

Divorce (or Not): A Guide

Part I: Divorce

~

A Guide to Divorcing with Wisdom, Sanity, and Integrity

Joseph Shaub
Attorney at Law
Marriage and Family Therapist

Cover Design by David Moratto

First Volume Edited by Jennifer D. Munro

ISBN-13: 978-1530802005

ISBN-10: 1530802008

Printed in the United States of America by CreateSpace

To Bev, Dani and our beloved Buddy
Who brought me the blessings of family

Divorce is a savage emotional journey.

– Abigail Trafford

...there is a better way.

– *Constance Ahrons, PhD*

CONTENTS

Divorce (or Not): A Guide

Part I
DIVORCE
~
A Guide to Divorcing with Wisdom, Sanity & Integrity

INTRODUCTION

Welcome to the world of divorce and intimate conflict.

Why "welcome?" you might ask. Well, good question! It's the first of many I hope to answer in the course of this book.

You will find in these pages, an invitation to shift perspective. My hope is that you will take up this invitation and, in doing so, view the struggles so common at the end of an intimate partnership in an entirely new light.

We have been stuck for many years thinking about conflict and divorce in a way that leads us in one direction – down. Yet the brick wall of fixed beliefs and fearful self-defense that millions keep slamming into as they try to untangle the financial and emotional thickets of their failed marriage is often just a mirage. What we see as a substantial and frustrating barrier to a non-destructive dissolution need not exist.

If people who embark on this divorce journey were to draw a map of their expected path, it would likely be an inevitable, jagged, disconnected road. Worse yet, once setting out on this *haj to hell,* this *autobahn of anxiety,* they would find themselves driving in a thick fog, so it's hard to know if they are edging toward a 10,000 foot drop off or an easy-to-manage sloping shoulder.

Immersed in this fog, the traveler will listen to just about anyone who says they know how to get safely to the end. The old, wizened guide (with degrees on the wall) says he's guided people on this path many times before. "It's the route used by thousands *just this year!* And hey – it's pea soup out there. Are you going to try this on your own?" So, people trudge along this well-worn path thinking, "It's *got* to be the best way. Look how many people are on it."

What these struggling people don't realize is that, if the fog were to lift – if they could see clearly – the path they'd been on, with all those others, is a wreck. Well-worn grooves leading through swamps; potholes galore; bridges with black ice warnings (ignored because of low visibility) – you get the picture. They'd also see, to their amazement and relief, that for the last twenty five years, people have been building alternate routes, and maybe it's the fog, maybe it's those experienced guides who insist we take the path they learned when they were young, or maybe it's the fear of something different than the "norm," but darned few people are to be seen on these other paths.

So there you have it – the simple purpose of this book is *to lift the fog*.

There is a better way to divorce that doesn't require the mortgaging of your future and your kids' financial and emotional wellbeing. Even if you begin with deep feelings of hurt, anger and betrayal, the divorcing process, *itself*, does not have to exacerbate these feelings. It is *not* inevitable that you become permanently and grievously estranged from the person who had been your dearest intimate partner and, in most cases, the other parent of your children. Mediation and Collaborative Divorce are incredible creations. Each is a worthy refinement of decades-old methods of supporting people who struggle with the severing of a most cherished bond. I want you to know more about them. I want you to engage them.

In the following pages, I'll not only be imparting what I hope to be helpful information, I will also introduce you to Adam and Beth (our divorcing couple) and the people who shepherd them through the legal gauntlet. Our chapters will usually begin with a part of their stories. In doing this, I seek to reveal them as living, breathing examples of the material that will follow. Finally, each chapter will conclude with practical summaries, check-lists, and exercises.

There's a lot packed in here. My hope is that you will come away with new ways to think about your partner and yourself, your relationship, lawyers, courts, divorce, and unicorns. Okay, maybe *not* unicorns. That will be my next book.

A BRIEF PERSONAL STATEMENT

I became a lawyer in 1974. Seventeen years later, I was licensed as a marriage and family therapist. When I left full-time law practice to begin the master's degree program in marriage and family therapy, my Uncle Lennie, who was a wonderful guy, asked me, quizzically, "Why?" I couldn't answer him then in a way he—or even I—could understand. This book is my attempt, years later, to answer my dear uncle's question.

But first…I was a lawyer. The early years found me exploring various kinds of law and even leaving the practice for a while to become a bartender. Obviously, I hadn't found my fit. In the early eighties I was able to sink my teeth into an amazing kind of work. Even though many decades have passed since my involvement in what was known then as "DES Litigation," the experience remains pivotal in my professional life. It's actually a major reason I sat down to tap out this book on my computer. The story is worth recounting now. While it doesn't seem to have anything to do with divorce, please bear with me. The connection will unfold.

Back in the 1930s, Charles Dodds, a researcher in England, came up with the first synthetic estrogen, later known as "DES." In the dawning era of wonder drugs, it was considered a walloping breakthrough. Until then, women who needed estrogen replacement therapy had to endure a series of painful injections. Now, they simply had to swallow a pill each day.

Because DES was developed across the Atlantic, no one in America could slap a patent on it, so the drug was manufactured by more than 100 companies over the years. As still happens today, the drug companies kept looking for other medical problems that might respond to DES, in order to expand their markets. Physicians began to give this new wonder drug to pregnant women who had histories of miscarriage and others who were spotting or going into premature labor. DES saved many of these pregnancies, according to the doctors. A couple of researchers at Harvard ran a study that seemed to confirm these reports, thus opening the door for FDA approval. Thousands of doctors started prescribing this drug to pregnant women in the late 1940s and early '50s.

While the estrogen replacement therapy for post-menopausal women recommended dosages of 5 mg or 10 mg, this pregnancy-preserving regimen had prospective moms taking an increasing dose of the drug, peaking at 125 mg a day.

Decades passed. Then in 1971, Dr. Arthur Herbst, a cancer specialist, was struck by the coincidence of eight young women in their late teens to early twenties all being admitted to Boston General Hospital with an incredibly rare form of cancer of the vagina called *clear cell adenocarcinoma*. This devastating cancer had been seen (rarely) in older women, but never in this much younger population...*Ever*. The alarm bells that went off were heard all the way to California. Herbst conducted a thorough history and found that the one thing linking these unfortunate young women was their mothers' use of DES when pregnant with them. DES was ultimately yanked from the market for pregnancy support and, a few years later, some of the young women whose lives had been so horribly impacted filed lawsuits against the drug companies.

I was working in the 1980s for a Los Angeles law firm that represented a number of these women. In a word, DES litigation was fascinating. Almost without exception, I bonded with my clients and enjoyed working with them. The legal issues were wide, varied, and super challenging. It was a lawyer's dream. I spent many engrossing days in medical libraries and law libraries, in strategy sessions and in court.

Yet, there was a part of the whole process that was deeply troubling.

Every woman who brings a lawsuit like this must sit for a deposition, in which the lawyers for the other side will have her sworn in and ask her questions—lots and lots of questions. Many was the time that I would sit next to a wonderful, brave, and vital person in her late twenties and defend her as she was asked an entire day's worth of questions by a battery of a dozen lawyers (representing the major drug companies), almost all of whom were men. The women would be asked *everything*, from the most mundane elements of their personal history to a detailed exploration of their sexual history and even the kinds of menstrual periods they had. The rules of legal "discovery" allow these kinds of questions.

The process was absolutely brutal for the individuals who were sucked up into its gears. More and more, I observed that the only people who really won when lawsuits started were the lawyers. I saw that lawyers live in their own worlds when it came to litigation, and they were either unaware of, or didn't care about, how that process affected the parties. I became extremely disenchanted by the litigation process and chose to leave the practice and return to school to study therapy. I had positive experiences of my own in counseling and the draw was natural, the fit excellent.

Not wanting to waste years of law training, I spent the next number of years shifting my practice focus to family law. I was able to blend my dual professions well. Counseling clients through the monumentally painful process of divorce was gratifying. However, if I thought personal injury litigation was hard on people, I was often stunned by the insensitivity and downright mean-spiritedness of divorce litigation. I came to believe that conventional divorce litigation was equivalent to torture, and I even began using that word to describe what we family lawyers put people through. Over the years, my practice morphed naturally to performing divorce mediation services and also providing therapy to couples who wanted to preserve their relationships. Friends would joke with me that I'd try couples therapy and, if it failed, I'd take on the richer partner as a client in the divorce. Of course, that was impossible, and, in fact, I have long made it a firm policy to never wear more than one hat with any client. If I am a couples therapist and things don't work out, I refer them to mediation or collaborative lawyers. It keeps things cleaner for me and less confusing for people who are already struggling.

The mix of professions was tailor-made for the practice of divorce mediation, which I avidly pursued. Then, in the mid-90s, I read a riveting article by a San Francisco divorce lawyer named Pauline Tesler describing an incredibly elegant approach to legal dissolution called Collaborative Divorce. I thought, "What a fantastic idea! Only problem is, you need another lawyer to work with and nobody in Washington is practicing Collaborative Divorce, yet." Then, in 1999 it *arrived* in my adopted home state and I embraced it like a parched man welcomes an oasis—like a dog grabs a bone—like…well, you catch my drift.

Collaborative Law sprang from the mind of a brilliant and compassionate Midwestern lawyer and arose in the early 1990s. It captivated a vast swath of legal professionals who hungered for a pathway to guide people to a sane and decent outcome if their relationship ruptured. While divorce lawyers frequently complain about the deep emotional toll their practices exact upon them, the collaborative lawyers I know *love* what they do.

Yet, whenever I speak to people in the community, almost no one knows what collaborative law is and how radically it differs from the more conventional (and destructive) process of litigated divorce that's been practiced for decades. I hope that this offering will help remedy that.

Finally, a note on why this formerly one-volume offering is now split into two: I am fortunate to have been trained in two professions—

law and therapy. Themes which accompany relationship distress and then, later, dissolution of that relationship hang together like sustained notes throughout that entire trajectory. It seemed natural, therefore, to write a book that combined two related messages. First, it is possible to repair a bond that feels hopelessly broken. Second, if you cannot manage this, there is *definitely* a better way to divorce—a way that can insulate you from the common psychic wounds and insults visited by the conventional divorce process.

After completing the two-year-long process of writing and editing the volume, and getting it up on Amazon in August, 2015, I sat back to clear my head and pursue my couples therapy and mediation practice and enjoy the pleasure that Autumn in the Pacific Northwest brings. My intention was to wait until the flipping of the calendar to a new year, and then more actively promote the messages in the book. I opened the volume again in January intent on re-reading the book and coming up with my "elevator speech" to describe what it was about (as I considered bringing it into bookstores for readings, professional conferences, puppet shows, rock concerts and the like). I trust you know what an elevator speech is—the task of describing something significant (most commonly, what you do for a living…but it may also be a topic like collaborative divorce) in a succinct enough manner as to take no more time than an elevator ride.[1]

In re-reading the text, it began to occur to me that combining two themes in one book reflected disrespect for those who had made the decision to divorce. After all, if you had arrived at this most painful conclusion, often after a lengthy internal struggle, to then have to read about how you might be able to repair your bond felt off-putting and tone deaf. A person who has made the decision to terminate the bond does not want or need to hear that the relationship can be saved. While this is an understandably difficult message for the person who does *not* want the divorce, it is true, nonetheless. One thing I have come to accept after years of doing this work is that when one person has concluded that the relationship is over for them, their partner's task is not to convince them they are wrong, but, rather, to commence the challenging, yet necessary, journey of acceptance and healthy redirection of their own lives.

Thus, I have decided to break the two messages held in one volume into two books. Now *Divorce (or Not): A Guide* is a two volume set, with only minor adjustments to the one volume edition. The volume you hold in your hands will address "Divorce." The second volume will address "or (Not)" and contain a discussion of the pathway to mending a frayed bond, in which *both partners* may feel hopeless, yet *still maintain the desire to reconnect and heal the wounds of their longstanding anger or distance.* If you are headed down the path of divorce, it is important for you to know what you are getting yourself into and how you can do the least amount of damage to yourself, your partner and your children (this book). If you are both unsure, despite your pain, then it is important for you to explore a path to deepening and strengthening your relationship in order to move toward its repair (that book).

Certain themes run through both volumes—particularly the vital role that attachment plays, both in describing the distress that dogs us when our intimate relationship feels insecure and understanding the inner devastation that often accompanies divorce.

I hope you find helpful information, support, and a path to peace in this first volume of the set. Now…to *Divorce.*

CHAPTER 1

The Decision

<u>Adam and Beth</u>

The blonde woman, sitting alone and silent at the small table in an otherwise bustling Starbucks, twists the gold band she is wearing. Over and over the ring circles her finger as she stares at her laptop. The absent-mindedness of her fingers belies the intensity of her concentration, as her eyes scroll down the entries in her Google search for divorce lawyers. Beth can't quite believe she is doing this after fifteen years of marriage. If her hands weren't worrying her wedding band, they might be flung up in the air in a "What am I supposed to do?" gesture of surrender. But that would draw too much attention to her, and Beth has never been big on that sort of thing. Her husband, Adam, has always been the one more comfortable—sometimes too comfortable—with being noticed.

Beth isn't sure how she got here, in this crowd, alone, contemplating divorce. It's not like she and Adam have screaming fights or that he abuses her or drinks or has affairs or…any of that stuff. It's mostly that he's just "gone" and Beth doesn't know why he left or how to get him back. It's not for lack of trying, that's for sure. She's taken great pains not to be a nagging bitch. She'd heard Adam complain about the way his mother spoke to his dad and had promised herself that she would honor his sharing of childhood wounds by steering well clear of that kind of behavior. That wasn't a problem, really, since anger wasn't part of the tapestry of family life when she was growing up. In fact, her own mom and dad never had a disagreement, as far as she knew, and they were still together and seemingly content after forty-five years of marriage. That probably accounted for the touch of shame she felt in her throat as she gazed at her computer screen.

No, she made sure not to nag, or at least she tried, but she also was not going to be stoic and simply enable Adam's growing emotional shutdown. She tried to be as non-blaming and factual as she could. "We don't do anything together anymore," or "I feel I have lost you to your work." She'd want to understand him so she'd ask him questions. "Why don't you touch me the way you used to?" His reactions had filtered down over the years to a handful of predictable responses. There might be an exasperated, "I don't know what you're talking about." She had also come to expect the defensive, "What do you mean? We went out to dinner just last week!" He had begun deflecting her comments by suggesting she might want to consider taking antidepressants. She didn't dare tell him that she had been doing just that for the past nine months. In fact, come to think of it, there were a growing number of things that she didn't share with Adam—from her daily regimen of Zoloft to the sessions of confiding with her childhood friend Daisy about her loneliness to…well, to sitting here looking at websites of divorce lawyers. All she knows for sure about herself and Adam is that she is feeling increasingly (shockingly) hopeless, and he has been getting more irritable and distant and she does not know what to do about it.

As Beth is musing, Adam is returning to the office after a great lunch with his sales team. He never fails to enjoy these monthly get-togethers. He loves his work like Picasso loved colors (or women). For a few years, now, his happiest times have been at work—making his numbers, getting the accolades, opening his bonus check (that he loved to bring home to help Beth understand that all that time was for her and the family). Bill and Susie have invited him to join them after work for a beer, but just the invitation puts Adam in a foul state of mind. He wants to join them and he also knows that he'll hear about it from Beth when he comes home an hour later than usual. If it wasn't that, though, it would be something else. "You don't do this or that!" It's the drumbeat of his home life—has been now for years. Beth has become a downer. If she would just get some help, maybe take antidepressants or quit talking to her sob-sister Daisy, things would lighten up around the house. Beth mentioned seeing a couples counselor last month, but Adam doesn't see why they have to go to someone else to fix their marriage. They're not that messed up. They don't fight—like Paul and Leila—and, after all, no marriage is perfect. If all he has to worry about is Beth complaining from time to time, they can get through this patch. Anyway, he's got work and his mates there, he's got the gym where he religiously keeps himself fit, and he's got his kids. He's also got the luck to be with a woman who isn't nasty, like his mother, and who is great with Lilly (age thirteen) and Jason (age ten). Yeah, he can get through this, and eventually Beth will figure out whatever is bothering her. Adam looks up from his computer and smiles to see Susie coming through his door to talk about her monthly numbers. She's a rising star.

THE DECISION

It may come after that last, harsh exchange—or when you look at your tired, dispirited eyes in the bathroom mirror one morning. You may decide that you don't want to expose your children to any more years of bickering and lovelessness.

One thing is very likely. The decision doesn't suddenly arrive out of nowhere. You have tried it on for some time and whenever the notion of severing this bond has arisen, you have rejected it. You may step away from the decision to divorce for the kids—or fret about what your family or circle of friends might think about you—or be held back by a dark guilt that hovers above you constantly. *Hope*, against the evidence, for a change and better outcome—that most human malady—may guide you. Certainly, fear of a future of financial want or loneliness causes many to step back from the edge. Whatever the individual case, for all but the most impulsive (you, who need to jump without a parachute), the decision will come after a life's chapter marked by deep uncertainty and inner struggle.

Thus, when the decision is made, it usually arrives after a period of considerable contemplation. As such, it is firm and, in almost all cases, not subject to reversal. This is why, when a couple enters my office seeking divorce mediation assistance, if one partner has made the decision (over the resistance of the other), for all my personal and professional desire to help couples come together from a place of estrangement, I will not invite any discussion of reconciliation. This is because the personal journey to the divorce decision has been so fraught with pain and doubt, to disregard that person's firm, yet anguished, arrival at a decision is an affront to their psyche and personal integrity. When a partner is faced with the seemingly intolerable decision by the other to sever the bond, the task is not to reverse the decision—which I think needs to be acknowledged—but to help that partner struggling with overwhelming loss to incorporate this new reality, over time, into their life.

TWO DIFFERENT WORLDS
~ THE LEAVER AND THE LEFT ~

Divorce almost always starts on a different foot for each partner. At the beginning, it is not a mutual decision. One person leaves emotionally, and the other is left. One gets dumped, and the other is the dumper.

For the divorce initiator, it usually takes a while for you to cross that line. If you think of the decision to divorce as a wall you have to pass through, then you approach it and bounce off it a number of times. Then something happens. Maybe it's a heated fight where seemingly unforgiveable things are said. Maybe it's an admiring (and long-missed) look from a good-looking guy. It could just be rolling out of bed one morning and gazing in the bathroom mirror at your sad face. It could be anything…or nothing. However, one thing you *do* know is that *you are done*. Your emotional investment in your marriage is over. You have passed through that wall, and you can't pass back through.

You can think of that emotional disengagement like a campfire— an apt image for the Northwest, where thousands stream out of Seattle to sleep by mountains and lakes every year. A vibrant marriage is like that campfire late at night before you turn in. The flames are skipping and dancing. It is full of life. When you awaken the next morning and go to the fire pit, you see what is left of the logs that were ablaze the night before. They haven't been consumed entirely, but they lie there blackened and still. This represents the marriage after years of disconnection and bickering. If you lift one of the remaining log fragments, you might see spots that still have sparky embers embedded in the wood. If you blow on those embers hard and long enough, smoke will start to stream from the log until a flame pops out again. However, sometimes it has rained during the night. You come out and look at the wood, and it is dead. Turn the logs over and look underneath and it's just blackened, the flame long gone. That is the way a person feels when their emotional commitment to the marriage is over. It is just……done. Nothing by the partner—nothing they can do themselves—will bring it back.

Michele Weiner-Davis, marital therapist and best-selling author has coined the term "Walkaway Wife," and it's a great description of a phenomenon that therapists see in their offices every day. This is the end of the marriage within the woman's heart, and it often goes something like this:

She has been trying for years to connect with him. He says he doesn't understand what she wants and gets defensive or he withdraws. Whatever his reaction, her efforts to reconnect emotionally with her partner become more and more frustrated. One day she makes a decision, "When _____ happens, I'm gone." That blank is filled in with any number of things. "When the last child is out of the house…" "When I finish school…" "When I get a job…" "When I get my inheritance…" "When I lose thirty pounds…" Once that very internal decision is made, she becomes calm. She doesn't care any more whether he is present. She stops trying to connect. Since her efforts to reach out to her partner often felt like a barrage of criticism to him, he suddenly thinks that everything must be hunky-dory because the criticism has stopped. While she is done, he is relieved that the marital distress seems over and believes they are on a new and positive footing. So, obviously, when that day arrives and her contingency occurs—

when she says she's done and "adios"—he is understandably shell-shocked.

For the person who leaves (the "Dumper," as described by one author[2]), there might be a sense of relief that a decision has finally been made. It will almost always be mixed with sadness and regret—surely guilt for having made this decision to fracture a family. This guilt can be quite a burdensome weight on the heart. Usually, the person who has left has been struggling with the decision for a long time and has also been pondering what life beyond the marriage would be like. This person needs to move on to the next step in his life.

For the person who has been left (labeled the "Dumpee" by that same author), the experience is far, far different. First, and most importantly, the secure marriage, which had been propped up in his head by denial, is blown up. Now, there's nothing inherently bad or wrong about denial. Almost all of us resort to this internal defense when reality feels too much to bear. We can take this unpleasant truth, compartmentalize it, and do pretty well, paying attention to the other things that aren't painful. The biggest problem with denial is that when it is shattered, the drop is long and the landing hard. The Dumpee might think something like, "Well, the marriage wasn't great, but I thought we'd get through it. I thought it would be better when _____ (again, fill in the blank: when the last kids left the house, I got that promotion, she went back to work). So we had our problems…but *DIVORCE???*" While the Dumper might be struggling with guilt, the Dumpee is usually faced with a much wider spectrum of more intense feelings. Anger can come up. Betrayal, grief, or fear are common.

So people enter the divorce drama in vastly different places, emotionally. One is likely to be in a hurry to get done. This isn't out of disrespect for their partner, but more because they feel like they are hanging in limbo, which is a tough and unsettling place to hang. The other person is in exactly the opposite place. That person needs time to process through what is happening to them. Their life has just caved in on them, and they will need to sort out their feelings, their future, and their current needs—which is a tall order.

Adam and Beth

Beth will tell you that she was raised in a "normal" family. Her mother and father are still together after forty-six years of marriage.

Her sister, Joan, got divorced in her twenties after a brief "practice marriage," which then led to her wedding Nate three years later. They are still together and happy. While Joan (five years her senior) was social and only a little rebellious growing up, Beth was most decidedly the "good girl." She never knew anything less than an "A" throughout high school, served in student government, and was a strong, all-league defender on the girls' soccer team. She met Adam at a fraternity party her junior year at the U. He wasn't even in the fraternity, but while she made boring small talk with a succession of men, she couldn't help noticing the good-looking guy circulating and talking with a woman here, two or three guys there. He seemed engaging and charming, laughs and a sense of conviviality following him about the rooms where people were circulating. She didn't like drinking, so when the evening started to get louder it felt like time to ease away and return to her apartment—and then Adam appeared by her side out of nowhere. After they chatted for ten minutes, he told her he was tired of the noise and asked her if she'd like to go somewhere for coffee before they both called it a night. He seemed safe enough and he was certainly good looking enough, so they left together—and closed the local coffeehouse three hours later.

The two things she remembers, even years later, were how deep and dark his eyes were and how lively and intelligent his mind was. She had expected some smooth and shallow operator, but this guy thought about things—and he listened. They had a surprising amount in common, topping the list with outdoor activities, classical music, country dancing, and reading by a roaring fireplace. Within two weeks they were spending most of their time together and within four they were lovers. She told her best friend, Daisy, "Every time I see Adam, I just want to rip his clothes off." Daisy punched her, "You go, girl!"

Her last two years in college were a dream, and they moved in together right after graduation. The only bump in the road was the time Adam got into graduate school on the other end of the country, but Beth's father had been diagnosed with cancer and she told him she just couldn't move while he was going through chemo. Adam said that was fine and got his MBA from the state university, but he seemed to withdraw for a while after that. He came out of it, but she never understood what dark spirit seemed to enter him, because he didn't talk about it.

Their marriage came soon after and Beth settled in to a happy, secure life as a wife. She wanted desperately to start a family, but Adam said he wasn't ready. They didn't have enough money yet. Whenever the subject of money, or children, came up, Adam would shut down for what seemed days at a time. He wouldn't be mean or angry. He'd just be somewhere else. Before he earned his MBA, he'd already nabbed a job as a sales manager for a growing medical instrument company. Eventually, their first of two children came along and they settled into the pattern that would last for years. Beth stayed home for eight years until the baby, Jason, could handle daycare, and then she found work as a part-time bookkeeper. The stability of the lifestyle and the way the columns of numbers added up at the end of the day were all deeply satisfying to her.

Yet, while she was getting into a groove that fit her, Adam began to seem restless. She couldn't put her finger on it. They didn't fight. He was still an attentive, if not thrilling, lover, and he was a good dad—when he was around. There was a lot of travel with his work and when he was home, there was a lot of "care and feeding" of his sales force. He managed a local group and four others in the Western Region, so travel was definitely more frequent than she would have wanted.

As the years progressed, Beth became achingly aware that she was lonely. She appreciated all of Adam's hard work, so she didn't want to upset him, but she just couldn't keep it to herself. She wanted them to be a team, but it wasn't working out like that at all. She didn't want to make him feel pressured, so Beth tried hard to figure out the right words to use. She'd talk to Daisy and practice in the car. Yet, whenever she'd say things like, "Adam, I'm lonely," or, "You've changed," he'd either get defensive or irritable, and then would retreat to his office to go over the numbers. She offered to help, but he declined. He'd spend two hours or more in that room, and many was the night she'd poke her head in and say she was going to bed, hoping he'd join her. He seldom did. She didn't feel responsive to his sexual explorations and, eventually, they stopped having sex altogether. When they did, it sure didn't feel like making love, and she had come to a place where she could take it or leave it. Adam kept fit and she appreciated that about him, but the eyes didn't seem so deep anymore.

Beth began to feel her marriage slipping through her fingers. She asked Adam to go to couples counseling, but he didn't see the point. "There's nothing wrong with our marriage we can't fix ourselves." For a couple of years, he'd plan a "date night" after she would say something about being unhappy, but eventually he stopped and just got quieter and quieter. Yet, whenever she heard him talk on the phone with one of his poker buddies or salespeople, he'd be animated and chatty. Beth found herself focusing more time and attention on the two kids.

She and Adam had agreed that she could use her part-time income for whatever she wanted, so she decided to start seeing a therapist but not tell Adam. Week after week, she'd regale Delores with her stories of loneliness—the feeling that she and Adam were living parallel, disconnected lives that only came together around the children. One afternoon, she talked about her fear of dying alone and loveless and she broke into sobs, the intensity of which surprised her. She stopped trying to get Adam's attention. She began to find his kisses even repulsive.

Then, one morning, Adam told her that he was leaving that afternoon for a hastily scheduled four-day sales meeting at a ski resort in Utah, and something inside of her broke. There was a time she would have been irritated—even angry—but now she was just numb. After everyone had left for work or school, she called Daisy in a semi-panic and told her she had to see her. Over lunch that day, at the tail end of salads and a shared bottle of Pinot Gris, Beth realized she couldn't do this any longer. In the commonest of all statements, she wearily shrugged her shoulders and told Daisy, "I love Adam, but I'm not in love with him anymore." Then she uttered the words she'd prayed she'd never say, "I think I want a divorce."

Daisy told her to talk to her therapist about it and give it a week's thought, which Beth did. She couldn't understand it, she told Delores. Adam was a good man—a great father and solid provider. She was steeped in guilt. Yet, she had done everything she could: joined a gym and lost weight, bought sexy negligee, told him she needed him, not told him she needed him, taken antidepressants because her unhappiness was maybe her fault, and suggested on at least a half dozen occasions that they see a couples therapist.

None of this had made the slightest difference. She felt trapped. She felt that if she stayed in this marriage, she would die.

The day after Adam came home from his trip and she felt a black cloud descend over her life again, she could be found at the local Starbucks, twirling a wedding ring, searching for divorce lawyers.

TAKEAWAYS

- **If your spouse has chosen to end the relationship, you may feel many painful things: blindsided, betrayed, humiliated, among others. While *communication* of the decision may seem abrupt and out of nowhere, it probably has come after a long period of soul searching. It is important that, for all your pain, you do not resort to punishing your spouse for this decision.**

- **If you have left your marriage emotionally, be aware that your spouse will often be very alert for signs of a change of heart and a chance at reconciliation. Your efforts to be kind or let them down easy may be naturally interpreted as overtures to reconciliation and when you reiterate your decision to end the marriage you will be accused of sending mixed messages. It is best to be kind, yet firm and mindful of gestures that can be misinterpreted. Your effort to not be the "bad guy" may result in greater confusion and pain for your abandoned spouse.**

- **If you have decided to divorce, you may not have a good answer to "Why?" the question you can expect to get. This does not mean that you do not have your reason(s) but you are just unable to articulate them at this point. You will likely feel a great deal of guilt once you have arrived at the decision to divorce. Be sure not to be guided by this guilt in doing something that is inconsistent with your decision.**

- **If you have been left by an intimate partner you are faced with the universal life challenge of forgiveness. There are many excellent books discussing forgiveness by Spring and Luskin, among others, as well as an excellent lecture on** forgiveness by Kornfield. **If your partner is truly remorseful for the pain you are experiencing, this is your invitation to explore this path, not an invitation to discuss reconciliation.**

CHAPTER 2

Divorce in the 21st Century

Linda, the Divorce Lawyer

Linda was one of those people who *did* go to law school so she could help people. Of course, another factor was that by the time she had hit her senior year at the university, she hadn't a clue what she would do after graduation. Her major had been American Literature, so she left school with an overloaded bookshelf, moderate debt, and a handful of choices. She thought of traveling around Europe and maybe teaching English; sticking around home and working at her mother's catering business and starting the book that had been marinating in her brain for the last couple of years; entering graduate school in her field; or going to law school. She didn't know much about law school. Her father told her she could do a lot of things with a law degree and her mother said it was something she could always fall back on if the writing didn't pan out. She had taken the LSAT on a bit of a lark and scored in the 98th percentile.

It was a difficult decision. She had heard that a good approach would be to draw a line down the middle of a page (she even bought a yellow legal pad, because that just made sense) and list all the "pros" on one side and all the "cons" on the other. When she stared at the two columns, the one item on the "pro" side that said, "I can be of service to others" seemed to grow and change colors before her eyes, dwarfing all the other careful cursive adorning the page.

Linda was excited when she began law school, almost rubbing her hands together in relish at the coming "intellectual feast"—something she had heard someone say about studying the law. Almost from the start, though, her inherent optimism was challenged. First, she realized that it would be a long time until she could indulge her love for reading anything other than casebooks and legal analyses. Next, Linda became aware of how hard everyone worked to avoid the appearance of weakness. It seemed like every single one of these super bright and really nice people were petrified that they would ever look incompetent. Linda certainly felt that way. If she didn't respond in the crisp and articulate style required by her professors during a classroom exchange, she would feel an uncharacteristic depression descend upon her that evening. She welcomed the keggers that the law school sponsored on Thursdays and found that the buzz and goofing with her classmates were among the rare escapes from the pressure to excel.

She had never been around that many smart people in her life. While she was the only one to have read, much less loved, David Foster Wallace's doorstop *Infinite Jest*, she had classmates who had composed concertos, run businesses, and travelled the world (with a popular travel blog to show for it). She came to realize that working hard wasn't enough. That would put her right in the middle of the class or lower—and the chance of getting any kind of decent-paying job that would put a dent in her student loan balance would be remote.

By the time she had graduated, her mind honed razor sharp and in the top 20% of her class, Linda had in hand a job offer from a 25-lawyer firm. Her first two years of practice felt like a continuation of the hamster wheel—lots of late hours, lots of weekends, lots of "sorry I can't" to social invitations. Also, there seemed to be lots of tedium, with work on cases where the arguments were technical and always distilled to fights over how to move money around. That long-ago marquee on her legal pad about helping people didn't feel like part of her life. Then, she was asked to help on a divorce case for a business client—and she found her calling.

The case involved a twelve-year marriage and two kids (eight-year-old twins). Her office represented the husband, and their client's wife was trying to get a big piece of the business he had started and built up before he had met her. In Linda's first conference with their client, she was struck by his charming intelligence and vowed that she would not allow his soon-to-be-ex and her lawyer to wreck what he had devoted so much of his life to creating. The wife's lawyer was positioning her as having given up a potentially lucrative career as a businessperson, herself, as she had chosen to forego an MBA program, after a stellar undergraduate performance, to get married and start a family. She was attractive and their client was convinced that she would remarry the minute alimony was over. He wanted to be fair with her. He said that a lot and Linda believed him. It wasn't clear why the wife couldn't use all that intelligence now to get a job. What really got under Linda's skin, though, was the way she treated the twins as her possession, insisting that Linda's client get only alternate weekends with them. The more Linda got into this case, the more she felt impatient with the wife's arguments and the more she wanted to protect her client from the other lawyer.

The case never went to trial. It settled after an all-day mediation session. Her client walked out of the room at the end of the day with mixed emotions—relieved it was over and resentful about how his wife had put the screws to him. It could have been much worse, Linda knew, and she helped him get much more time with his twin sons than his wife wanted him to have.

She asked for more divorce cases and, within six months, she was one of the two lawyers in the firm practicing only domestic relations. Her first trial lasted a week and was exhilarating. Cross-examining the other side's vocational expert was the most fun she had ever had as a lawyer. She saw how hard divorce was on people and believed she was the only thing standing between her clients and an angry, or manipulative, or lying soon-to-be-ex-spouse. Plenty of times, the people getting divorced seemed to get along well, and they were able to reach an expeditious settlement and keep the costs of divorce down to the low-to-mid five figures. She liked those cases. She felt like she was shepherding people through a dangerous passage—sort of like Ulysses in the book she had loved in college. She was helping people. She just had this wish that they'd seem more appreciative.

WHY LEGAL DIVORCE IS SO HARD ON PEOPLE
Dirty Laundry — Turning Love into Hate

Think about the process. Two people are trying to get a third person, who is wearing "the black muumuu" (the judge, in the words of an old friend), to make a decision in their favor:

Bill doesn't want to pay as much alimony as Jane wants, so he argues that she can go to work now (even though she's been out of the workforce raising kids for the last dozen years).

Ruth has been home with the children, now six, eight, and twelve, and feels vigilantly protective of them, as Ralph has left her and is now dating another woman. She outlines her strengths and Ralph's deficiencies as a parent in objective terms—after all, she's been there and he's been working long hours over those years.

Maury took $100,000 from the money he inherited when his father died and used it as the down payment on the house he and Diane bought after they got married. Twelve years later, they are separating and he wants that money back, but Diane argues that he put the money into a house in both of their names and after twelve years it is no longer his separate money.

For every legal dispute that lawyers might find "interesting" or "challenging," there is a pair of regular people who are worried about their futures. Suddenly they find themselves fighting with the person who at one time had been their closest love. Even the most factual statement—leached of emotion and accusation—when put in a public record in a divorce proceeding in court, will hit an exposed emotional nerve. It's important to know that you don't have to say anything dramatic or nasty to wound this other person.

Few divorce cases ever go to trial—far less than 5%. Yet, that doesn't mean people don't go to court.

When you file in court for divorce, you aren't going to get a trial date for many months, sometimes as much as a year or more. Lots of divorce cases don't settle until people are "at the courthouse steps." So, what happens when people have disagreements about what to do during this in-between period? Sarah needs a certain amount to cover her expenses and hasn't worked in years, but Bill doesn't feel he can afford to give her as much as she says she needs. Norm wants to be with his children as much as possible, but Rachel only feels comfortable letting them be away with their dad for a day every other weekend. Who stays in the house? Who drives the Suburban? Is Dad an alcoholic and inclined to drive with the kids after a few? Is Mom?

These are among the barrelful of questions, arising at the beginning of a legal divorce, which have to be answered. If the divorcing people can't work it out, they have to put it before the person sitting on that high bench to make the decisions for them. These are "motions for temporary orders," and that's where the action is in divorce, as far as being in court is concerned. Mostly these things get decided based on written statements under oath that each spouse gets to read and respond to. I would hate to be in the tummies of the people who read the statement from their divorcing spouses for the first time…not to mention their spouse's family and friends. One expert in divorce and children called this lining up of support "tribal warfare."[3]

The doctor is at home in the examining room. The teacher is comfortable in the classroom. Construction workers can perch on girders and eat their lunches. The writer tolerates, even enjoys, hours of solitude. None of these people wants to be in court. Courtrooms are alien to all but the lawyers who do their work there day in and day out. The poor divorcing party will stand next to their lawyer and listen to the case that is being made for and against them and feel utterly exposed. They will hear statements they feel are demeaning, dismissive, denigrating, and *untrue*, made in public, and they will think, "*This* is what it has come down to? I am in combat with my husband/wife?" I have seen such forlorn resentment on the faces of people forced into this macabre public theatre.

You are trying to convince a stranger that what *you* are asking for should be granted. Maybe the fact that your husband is habitually late is an important factor that will sway the judge. There was the time that your wife was nervous about a doctor's exam and got too drunk at a party and made a fool of herself. Thinking about it, maybe she needs that glass of wine with dinner too much. She *absolutely* disagrees with her husband that their two-year-old can be put facing forward in the car seat; suddenly this feels like the child is not safe with him. Spending habits come under scrutiny. He spends too much on golf. She didn't have to take those trips with her girlfriends. You think, "How *dare* they bring this up!" You also worry, "Is this going to make a difference? Am I going to end up with less support than I need? Will I be blocked from being with my kids except for a tiny window of time?"

Now, bear in mind, that these are fears that arise when normal divorce cases are going to court, brought by lawyers who are decent people, not interested in causing undue distress. There is a small percentage of lawyers in every city and town who don't work like that. They think it is their job to throw as much dirt as they can at the other spouse, and the arguments in front of the judge consist of one verbal grenade after another being lobbed at the other side. It's nasty. This takes a painful experience and amps it up so that it rocks a person back on their heels.

On top of this, the time has now come that people, for a small fee, can sit at a computer in their pajamas in the middle of the night and search court files at home. Potential bosses, lovers, and rivals can scan your divorce file. Adult children can read in wonder and dismay what their parents said about each other in public years earlier. In a world of shrinking privacy, our most searing pain is *public* pain.

Legal "Discovery" — Lots of Haystack/Not Much Needle

Once you've got these temporary court orders in place and some kind of status quo is established until everything is wrapped up months in the future, the lawyers then start on their voyage of discovery.

"Discovery" refers to the ways that a lawyer can find out what she needs to know in order to go to trial or settle the case. The most common kind of discovery is a set of written questions that is mailed to the other side, called "interrogatories." These can go on for pages and pages, with many questions with sub-parts and sub-sub-parts. You are asked about events years ago. You'll look at some of these questions and ask, "Are they *serious?*"

Some lawyers ask about every detail of employment, including the business, income, benefits, supervisor, job duties, and anything else that might be found in your employee file for each year going back two, five, or even ten or more years. You will be asked about all houses you bought during the marriage, including date and price of purchase, mortgage, date and amount of sale, and amount received after closing and use of these funds. There might be requests for bank records going back many years. The same goes for credit card records. While this information for a certain period of time is necessary to understand peoples' *current* situation, lawyers feel compelled to extend the period of scrutiny so far back that the real motivation can only be harassment or uncovering fraud. Fraud and financial manipulation are rare, and the overwhelming majority of people getting divorced have a basic trust in the honesty of the other. "Why is she asking me all of this?" is a natural and frequent refrain. Many of these sets of questions can run up to 100 items with sub-parts and cover almost every conceivable area of life. It is an incredibly stress-inducing and alienating process.

SIDEBAR:
~THE FIRST MEETING WITH YOUR LAWYER~

When you first meet your lawyer, you are likely to hear that they will "protect" you. All of these questions lobbed at the other's feet, gathering all conceivable information, do have that protective feel. However, you've got to ask: Protect me from what? Protect me from whom? At the start of any conventional divorce, you get this strong message: "I will protect you from your spouse."

Many is the person who emerges from an introductory meeting with a lawyer torn up inside. You want to get divorced, but the message seems to be that it can't be done without an aggressive approach. You don't want to do battle. That has never been your relationship, but if they're going to do it to you, you've got to "protect" yourself. Some feel swept up into this current of conflict. Others decline to proceed this way, but it takes a strong person to question an "expert" in a field we know little about. There's nothing wrong with shopping for a lawyer. Check out their websites. You can learn a lot about their philosophy and approach there. A Cincinnati lawyer starts her website off with this: *You deserve personal attention for your unique situation. We are committed professionals who work as a team to provide you with the support you need.... This is an emotional time for you, and you need experienced assistance in making legal decisions that will affect you*

---

and your children's future. We listen to what you want and craft a solution to meet your needs.

A Connecticut lawyer by contrast warns: *Selecting the right family law attorney is one of the most important decisions you could make in your Connecticut divorce or child custody case. You want the right personal fit, especially because the personal stakes can be so high. If you have a controlling spouse, a partner who would hide assets, or children who are going to be used as pawns in a custody dispute, or you were just served with divorce papers out of the blue, you need to retain legal counsel to protect you and your children. And if your spouse is on a mission to take everything and leave you with nothing, you need somebody on your side.*

One Washington lawyer promotes his "scorched earth" approach to divorce with a picture of a flaming mushroom cloud. So the approaches can vary widely.

Never hesitate to ask questions upon your first meeting. See if they can talk to you in person for fifteen to twenty minutes at no charge. Find out how much of their practice is family law (100% domestic relations practice, versus part divorce, part personal injury, part criminal defense can tell you a lot about this person's familiarity with the intricacies of family law and openness to non-litigated approaches to representation and counsel).

Find out how much work this lawyer will be doing (as opposed to other lawyers in their firm or legal assistants) for you. How available will they be if you contact their office? How much do they talk? How much do they listen? There needs to be a good fit for you, so do your homework and assert yourself. Remember, when their work is done, they will be moving on to the next matter. You will be living with the result (and your ex-spouse) for years to come.

Back to Discovery: Not only will you be expected to answer scores of written questions and provide many pages of documents, you might also get to have your deposition taken. In a deposition, you sit in the other lawyer's office, with a court reporter taking down every word you say. You are sworn in and can be questioned for a few hours. It can be just one or two hours, or it can be the better part of a day. You are unlikely to be "grilled," although that does occur. Most lawyers are courteous and are just trying to get information, but there are a number whose interpersonal skills are, let us say, in deficit, and they do seem to be oblivious to your discomfort at best—and, in rare instances, to revel in it at worst. After all, you *are* the "opposing" party. One thing that's for sure about depositions—they are quite expensive. If your lawyer is taking the deposition of your spouse, then paying for your lawyer's time—to prepare for the thing, take the thing, and read the transcript of the thing later—*and* for the stenographer who sits there recording the thing, will run into the thousands of dollars. If you are the one having your deposition taken, there is a whole set of fees and expenses you will incur as well. Ultimately it comes out of the same pot of resources and, unless you are wealthy, it's a hit to your bank account. You'll always want to do a cost-benefit analysis if this is part of the plan of attack proposed by your lawyer.

To understand why all this "discovery" exists, a good place to start might be a story about Abraham Lincoln. Back in the day before he entered politics, Lincoln was a famously successful trial lawyer. Maybe his most legendary trial was the "Almanac Trial," where he was defending the son of a close family friend from a murder charge. The victim had been bludgeoned to death at around midnight. One witness claimed he saw the accused commit the foul deed from about 150 feet away. On cross-examination, Lincoln asked how he could identify the assailant from such a distance, and the reply was, "By the light of the moon." At that point, Lincoln the lawyer whipped out an almanac showing that at midnight on the night in question, the moon was in its new phase, riding low on the horizon. The scene of the crime was bathed in *zero* light. An acquittal was won, and the case entered the Lincoln legend.

This was how cases were tried in the nineteenth and most of the twentieth centuries. Artful cross-examination, surprise, and counter-attack were engaging theatre, but there was also a problem: You never knew what the other side's case was until you heard it from the witness stand at trial. You might have a great case or a disastrous case, but you'd have to go to trial to find out. With any luck, you'd garner a Lincoln-sized coup. So, lots of cases would go to trial because lawyers didn't know if they had a good case or a bad case.

In the 1960s, states began passing laws permitting "discovery" by the methods described here. The idea—a good one, you might agree—was that a thorough understanding of the other side's case (and the evidence they had to support it) would encourage settlement and cut down on the mushrooming number of trials that were beginning to tax the court system. Yet, over the years, discovery became the most expensive part of any lawsuit. Stories are legion about businesses responding to requests to produce documents by inviting teams of young lawyers to spend as much time as they needed in warehouses filled with boxes containing millions of documents. The same arduous, time- and retina-taxing process is duplicated now with billions of bytes of information in computer files.

Interrogatories in divorce have been transformed into an inexpensive way to run up the other side's attorney fee bill, since all it takes is printing off a set of questions that are sitting in the lawyer's computer already. Change the names, take out a few questions that might not apply, and add a few that do, and, *voila*, a paper grenade is ready to be launched. I can say with some degree of confidence that anyone who has ever received these detailed inquiries, asking for information the other person either already knows or doesn't need, is more than a little aggravated by the time and effort required to respond. The discovery process does *not* make people getting divorced happy with each other.

The Settlement Conference — Modern Trial by Ordeal

So each side's lawyer amasses all the information they need. Nobody wants to go to trial. How do you get this thing settled? Here's the question asked another way: How do you settle this case in a manner that increases the odds that at least one person (and probably both) will feel drained, irritated, and dissatisfied when it's all over? It's a worthwhile question, because that is the predictable outcome of the system that has evolved.

First, you make sure that the people are separated during the process so they can't see the other *person* they are dealing with. There is a myth among most divorce lawyers that you can't put divorcing people together in the same room, because they are likely to start an emotional fire that will become uncontrollable. The settlement conference professional (a retired judge or experienced lawyer, usually) will go between conference rooms, meeting for as much as an hour at a time with each person and their lawyer, trying to move people closer together. "Closer together from what?" you might ask. Good question.

Before everybody meets, each side's lawyer puts together a collection of materials, often in a set of three-ring binders that contain all the important documents (again, usually a fraction of what was dug around for and handed over in discovery). All of this is preceded by a lawyer's letter laying out their client's case in the light most favorable to them...more happy reading for each person. The conventional wisdom of negotiation is like so: If you want 50 of something, you ask for 200 of that something in your opening bid. This makes sense. My long-ago mediation trainer, John Lemmon (no relation to John Lennon or Jack Lemmon), used to say there are basically two kinds of negotiation, "Middle Eastern Style" and "Swedish Style."

Middle Eastern Style negotiation is the conventional back-and-forth we have in mind when we think of negotiation. I want to sell you my used car. I want $10,000 for it, but I'll take $7,000. You don't want to spend more than $5,000, but you'll pay as much as $8,000. Right there, we figure the car will sell for somewhere between $7,000 (the lowest I'll take) and $8,000 (the most you'll pay). What will you offer for the car to start out? Well there *is* a lot of mileage on it and the interior is a bit worn...so you'll offer $3,000. "$3,000?" I reply. "I don't think so. Here is the service log that shows it has been babied like one of my own children. I'm not even sure I want to sell it, but if I can get $12,000, I'll let it go." You come up to $5,000, I come down to $10,000. I really want to sell it. You like the car and want to drive away in it. Maybe we haggle a bit more or maybe we just split the difference and agree to $7,500, and I hand you the keys.

You might not feel comfortable with this "game." If you don't negotiate for a living, this whole scenario might stress you out. You might prefer to engage in Swedish Style negotiation. You come to my home and look my car over. You figure in your head that these kinds of vehicles usually sell for somewhere between $5,000 and $10,000, depending on this or that. You can live with the midrange of $7,500, so you cut to the chase and offer $7,500 as your first, last, and best offer. The chances of our concluding a sale at that price are slim if the seller is an experienced negotiator.

Why should that be? After all, it's what we would have come to with a lot of back-and-forth haggling. The reason this style usually doesn't work is that in order for negotiations to conclude successfully, each side must feel that the other made some concessions. (This doesn't count if both sides hate negotiating and want to avoid that process. Then they will try to come to an agreement quickly and avoid the discomfort. This doesn't describe lawyers, who are professional negotiators. In fact, *negotiation is a far more frequently used skill by lawyers than courtroom advocacy*.) If I negotiate a lot, then I am *very* comfortable seeking some concession from the other person. So, your starting the negotiation with a final offer seems a bit arrogant to me. If you are making only one offer to me, you are asking *me* to make all the concessions. Any concessions you have made in your mental calculations have been inside your head. I don't see them, so I don't experience them as concessions at all.

Let's just say that I learned this lesson the hard way in my early days as a lawyer. Way back when, they didn't teach negotiation in law school. When I joined the legal workforce and started trying to negotiate auto accident settlements with experienced insurance adjusters, *I was eaten alive*. I would sanctimoniously make a Swedish Style and highly reasonable first, last, and best offer, and it would never—ever—be accepted. That's just not how experienced negotiators operate. Since I had already locked myself in, I couldn't move and keep face and credibility. It took me a few of these breakdowns to change my style. This is how "positional bargaining" works, and it is the dominant kind of negotiating in conventional lawyering.

Let's return to the divorce settlement conference. What will the experienced divorce lawyer put in her opening offer? Well, she's no Swedish Styler, so she will start out somewhere that gives her and her client a lot of room to move. Say you're a mom who has stayed at home with two children, who are now five and eight, while your spouse worked long hours and, thus, wasn't home much except for dinner, bedtime, and parts of weekends. You definitely think the children should live primarily with you. You feel a little uncomfortable about the children spending many overnights with their dad, but you understand that it is inevitable. However, you ask that the opening proposal be alternate Friday nights with Dad, returning to you at 5:00 p.m. on Saturday, and two hours for dinner every Wednesday.

Switch sides—you are a dad who worked his butt off to provide for this family. In fact, it was your spouse who decided she wanted the divorce, so you aren't feeling that darned charitable toward her anyway. However, you know that she's been the major parent so far for the kids, and dads don't fare that well in court. You could live with alternate weekends, as long as they start on Friday night and end on Monday morning. Yet, there's a part of you that doesn't see why you shouldn't have 50% custody. You're their father, for goodness sake! So, your opening gambit is to make the point that 50/50 custody is reasonable.

Both sides have given themselves room to move. It's probable that after some back and forth, they might end up with an agreement. But this is *divorce*, and fear, anger, defensiveness, and loss almost always come with the territory. It is nearly impossible to read an opening offer without reacting emotionally. How does the father feel about the mother who starts off by saying she is only comfortable with his having one overnight with his children every two weeks? How does the mother feel about the father who suddenly wants to have her little babies half the time, after she has been caring for them, from doctors to feeding to clothes to daycare to play-dates? My God, he doesn't even know the names of the children they play with every week!

Let us multiply this sense of umbrage around division of marital assets or payment of support. The normal steps in negotiation are now hobbled, as they are draped in reactions of outrage and betrayal. Countless are the hours that a settlement conference official spends trying to talk one, or both, of the spouses off the ceiling. The day feels endless. You start at 9:00 a.m., and by 5:30 p.m. (having had a brief break to wolf down lunch) you have both moved closer, but you haven't agreed to all the terms, and the ones with the greatest emotional weight might still remain unresolved. Do you walk away without an agreement? It has been a long day, and a lot of money has been spent. Are you actually going to throw whatever progress you *did* make into the trash heap?

_____

Most won't let that happen, and, by the end of the day, drawn and spent people end up "splitting the difference just to get it done" and avoid the dreaded trial. That's a pretty common solution. Does it sound like these people are anywhere close to satisfied? No, it doesn't to me either.

Then the day-after remorse hits. You wake up and the first thing that enters your mind is likely *not*, "Thank goodness it is settled. I can now move on." No, the first thoughts are about what you lost. The natural inclination is to obsess over what you gave up. This is quite natural. It is "loss aversion," legal-style.

LOSS AVERSION
IN A NUTSHELL

Many years ago, psychologists Amos Tversky and Daniel Kahneman found after a series of studies that the pleasure of winning is *far* outweighed by the pain in losing. For example, if you ask a group of people whether they would rather be given $100 or have a chance of picking 1 of 10 envelopes, 9 of which are empty and the other containing $1,000, the overwhelming majority would take the sure $100. Yet if you ask the same group if they would rather pay $100 or pick 1 of 10 envelopes, 9 of which are empty and the other containing an obligation to pay $1,000, the overwhelming majority would take their chances with the 10 envelopes, preferring the 9 in 10 chance of paying nothing. What accounts for the difference is "loss aversion." People will much prefer to avoid any loss. We become preoccupied with our losses. So, there is a natural tendency in most of us to ruminate on recent losses much more than to bask in the satisfaction of gain.

So, after the settlement conference, rather than be appreciative of the resolution and what was gained, you remember the lawyer telling you how much money you'd spend if you hadn't agreed yesterday. You wonder whether it was worth it. You think about your losses. Having been given no time to process through your gains and losses and come to terms with the *end* achieved, you will likely ruminate on the recent loss—imposed under pressure, as you now recall it. How do you think you will feel about your spouse at that point? If you are like most people, the answer is, "Not good."

_____

This is how the resolution of the legal divorce, as commonly experienced by people, will leave you feeling.

Fighting Over the Kids — Congratulations, You Have All Lost

What if you can't agree on a plan for parenting the kids? What if Mom is just too concerned about the outcome that Dad says he wants, and her protective instincts overwhelm her and she just can't agree? What if Dad has convinced himself that his donation of 50% of the genetic material for these kids entitles him to 50% custody? Well, what do you do now? You've got to find someone else to make the decision for you. Welcome to the world of the Parenting Evaluation.

It *could* be the most stressful experience you have in your life. You have agreed to be at the mercy of someone you do not know. This person will make a recommendation to a judge that will determine your relationship with your children for as long as they are minors. There's a lot on the line, and the person who is applying the pressure is none other than your soon-to-be-ex-spouse. Everything…*everything* that happens…every step along the way might well impact this most vital of all decisions in your life.

First, the evaluator will review all the papers that have been filed in court to get an idea of what is going on. Everything that your spouse said about you that made your stomach clench (and vice versa) is going to be read and tentative conclusions will be drawn, one way or the other.

Next, you will be interviewed, usually at length, by the evaluator. You'll be asked about your life story (all the time wondering if you should admit or omit something because it will bias this person), the history of your marriage, what's good about your spouse's parenting, what concerns you have, your history of alcohol and drug use, therapy/mental health treatment, your own strengths and struggles as a parent, and much more. All in all, you're likely to feel awfully exposed and vulnerable to another's judgment.

The next stage is commonly a visit to your home so the evaluator can observe you and your children interacting. He or she will want to meet with your children, often in their rooms. As much information will be gathered as possible, without asking the child who they want to live with.

This is followed by interviews of people who might know something about you and your parenting. Kids' teachers, doctors, your friends or relatives—any combination of these people will comprise the handful of "collateral contacts" who will be…well, contacted.

Somewhere in there, you might be asked to complete a set of psychological tests. You have no idea what these are supposed to show, so you will be forgiven for showing up a little paranoid in the results. (One commonly used instrument, the MMPI-2, has, among its many measurements, a paranoia scale, and it *is* expected to be a tad elevated in the course of a process that feels like a judgment on your fitness as a parent.)

When all this is completed, the evaluator writes a long, single-spaced report, which summarizes all of the steps described above, followed by a set of recommendations. Judges tend to rely heavily on these recommendations, unless you have hired a lawyer who is an expert at picking apart these reports. Even if you do, a good, experienced evaluator's report is usually "bulletproof" and will be almost completely adopted by a judge.

So how are you feeling at the end of this process? Maybe pissed? Righteous? Righteously pissed?

And who is the person who has put you through this? The other parent.

The point being that the parenting evaluation is a process that is virtually guaranteed to profoundly alienate parents. Resentments will deepen. Emotional walls will become thicker and more impregnable. It will be difficult to speak of, or think of, the other parent without experiencing that hurt and anger. The thing of it is, kids can sense it. Many is the parent I have heard say, "I have *never* spoken badly about the other parent in front of the kids, and we have been careful not to argue in front of them." Yet, despite these parents' care not to expose their children to the more overt behavior in their conflict, there is no way children can be shielded from their parents' actual feelings. As we will see later, exposure to parental conflict (overt or unexpressed yet present) is, far and away, the greatest stressor for children of divorce.

Research has repeatedly shown that most communication is nonverbal (one often-cited study out of U.C.L.A. states that *93% of communication is nonverbal)*. From our earliest months, we only had the capacity to read our caregivers' nonverbal communications. There is a basic tendency, as well, to trust nonverbal communication more than the verbal, in children as well as adults. When there is a conflict between verbal and nonverbal communication, children find this extremely confusing. Try as you might, you can't erase the information your child picks up from you nonverbally by denying the message with a spoken message.

The evaluation process concludes with a detailed, lengthy report. While it isn't a judge's ruling, it is about as close as you might get, knowing that a judge will likely adopt the report in her order (if the case goes to trial). Reading this appraisal of your strengths and weaknesses as a parent...as a *person*...is one of life's truly challenging experiences. Simply put, you don't want to subject yourself to this if you can help it.

Trial — The Bitter End

Some divorcing couples ultimately find themselves unable to come to an agreement about the terms of their divorce. These poor people end up in trial. There really isn't much to say about divorce trials, because they are so obviously costly, both financially and psychologically. An extremely small percentage of divorce cases go to trial—far less than 5%, thankfully. For those who end up before a judge, they have found themselves at the end of a long, costly, and extremely soul-sapping road.

For lawyers, trial is a *rush*. It is the ultimate in the "flow" experience, as a ten-hour day seems to pass in an instant. The most fun I ever had practicing as a lawyer was in trial. There are few, if any, dramatic moments. These unlikely events are reserved for television and movies and, very, very occasionally, real life. Nonetheless, every moment, every nuance and every indication of a judge's leanings, will result in an experience of ultimate engagement for lawyers.

For the clients involved with this experience, a major hazard of trial is the incomprehensibility of the result to at least one, if not both, people. The question is repeated many times daily in courthouse hallways throughout the country: "What just happened in there?" is the plea from a divorcing person who just got wiped out by a judge's ruling. For all the lawyer's experience and careful explanations, there's no way to help a client, who thought their cause was righteous, understand how they lost. Judicial decision-making is a crapshoot—an argument that lawyers will generally pull out on the eve of trial to encourage settlement. This is not to say that judges' decisions are inexplicable. It's just that we don't know what little morsel of fact that we thought insignificant will mushroom in importance inside the judicial brain. Why one person finds a particular fact deeply important and another dismisses it as insignificant can't be explained, but this truth about idiosyncratic thinking makes trial a risky venture (as well as being ungodly expensive).

This is the short description of conventional divorce as practiced in this country. The lawyers who ply this trade are overwhelmingly good people. Despite the mistaken legend to the contrary, most of them went to law school to help people. Those who find themselves practicing family law are even more likely than other specialists to want to help people. Why is it, then, that this work is so psychologically destructive to those poor souls who are experiencing the legal divorce? It's because the system itself is broken. Every incentive drives people over the cliff. To understand how this perpetuates itself, we must understand the *Seven Cardinal Rules of Legal Divorce*.

TAKEAWAYS

- **It bears repeating—vet your lawyer by reviewing their website and see if you can get a free consult to see if it is a fit. If the lawyer is reluctant, ask if you can meet, at least, for a free twenty minutes.**
- **Have all your questions about the lawyer's approach and philosophy written out before your first meeting and make sure they get answered.**
- **Make a self-assessment and decide how much you honestly need to "punish" your spouse for hurtful actions taken. Know that the more you need this retribution or justice, the greater your expense will be, <u>by a large factor</u>.**

- Understand an old, and widely accepted, adage among lawyers that people end up finding the lawyer who will match their personality and approach. Thus, if your spouse is angry, vengeful, or unreasonable, expect that their lawyer will be a reflection of that attitude.
- If you take the litigated divorce route, make sure you are an informed consumer, and work to understand every step in the process, its rationale, and the justification for the cost.
- Before you embark on a litigated divorce path, I hope you can stay with the remainder of this book to see if the alternative might be possible.

CHAPTER 3

The Seven Cardinal Rules of Legal Divorce

Beth

Beth had been surprised by two things when she told Adam she wanted a divorce. One was his angry reaction. They had been disconnected for so long—and he seemed happy with every part of his life but her—that his sullen and resentful withdrawal felt like an ambush. Then, to put the cherry on it and totally befuddling her, she looked at the email on his computer one night and saw that he had a months-long string of affectionate, flirty exchanges with Susie from the office. These combined to put Beth in a decidedly shaky emotional condition as she sat in the well-appointed waiting room of her lawyer.

She liked Linda from what she read on her firm's website. Linda had practiced family law for twenty-five years and had her own practice after working for a prominent local firm for ten years. She liked that Linda had a personal statement in her profile that said she

Divorce (or Not): A Guide
Part I

loved to read on rainy winter days and hike local trails with her dog, and she was a patron of the local symphony. The first conversation had been with Linda's assistant, Maggie. It had been pleasant, businesslike, and filled with detailed inquiries about finances and personal concerns. Beth was relieved to be welcomed by Maggie at the reception desk and to learn that she would be sitting in on this first meeting.

After she got settled in the conference room and sipped the steaming dark-roast coffee Maggie had brought her, Beth looked up when the door opened. An attractive woman in her early fifties, with short-cropped dark brown hair, wearing a stylish business suit, and carrying a laptop and a glass of water, entered the room. Linda had a calm yet commanding presence, and almost immediately Beth felt herself relax a bit.

After asking if it was okay to take notes on a laptop, Linda raised the lid, fixed her reading glasses that had been hanging from a black lanyard around her collar, and got down to business. She went through the intake information given to Maggie, checking for needed corrections and augmentations. After about a half-hour of rechecking and seeking additional personal and financial demographics, Linda closed her laptop, moved it aside, and looked directly at Beth. "How are your kids doing?" she asked. Beth was surprised and pleased by the question, as her children were her overriding concern. She told Linda that she was particularly worried about Adam's strange, "almost bipolar" response to her announcement that she wanted out of the marriage. She confided her worries that this Susie might be introduced into her children's lives and that she might even lose them to her. "I know that sounds ridiculous, but that's what scares me."

Linda was reassuring and told her that no judge would refuse a request for an order keeping a new partner away from the children, at least while the divorce was proceeding. She told Beth what she might expect for custody, child support, and alimony. Linda had seen hundreds of divorces and had a good feel for how judges were ruling in the local court. Beth left Linda's office with a welcome sense of calm and confidence. This lasted for exactly forty-eight hours.

That was when Beth received a call from Maggie, expressing her disappointment and informing her that Adam's lawyer had just sent a fax rejecting all of Linda's proposals for a temporary agreement. Could she come in some time in the next day or two and help them begin to prepare papers for a court motion? Beth received an email with a number of attachments, one of which was a detailed budget sheet requiring her to figure out how much she spent every month. Another was a notice that Adam's lawyer was going to subpoena the records of her therapist, Delores. "Why is he doing this?" Beth asked Maggie in a panic.

"Well," replied Maggie, "that's pretty much standard operating procedure when custody is at issue."

"What?" yelped Beth. "What do you mean, 'custody is at issue'? What does that even mean? Does he want the kids?"

"Don't worry. Really, Beth. Adam is pressing for 50/50 custody so you'll agree to lower alimony. It's typical negotiation strategy. He won't get it. Anyway, we are going to ask for the court to appoint a custody evaluator who will definitely come out in your favor based on your history. Um, and I've got to ask you, is it possible for you to put another $5,000 in our trust account? Your initial deposit will be used up by the time the hearing on these temporary orders is over."

Beth couldn't help herself. She got off the phone and called Adam at his office. "What the fuck are you doing?" she spit into the phone.

"What do you mean?" Adam asked, taken aback. Beth told him what she had just learned, and Adam said that was just his lawyer and he had nothing to do with it. He'd call his lawyer right away. Adam never called Beth back. There was no change from his lawyer. His communications became clipped and businesslike. When Beth read the statement that Adam had signed under oath and submitted to the court for their hearing for temporary orders, she was stunned and dismayed. He made comments about her possible mental instability and use of Zoloft for depression. He talked about how the economy was in transition, His income was going to be cut by 40%.

Beth was happy the Visa bill still went to her house, because she saw that he had taken a week off last month to be in Hawaii. That certainly went in her papers.

Through it all, Linda and Maggie were supportive and professional. The hearing was dreadful. Seeing Adam—stone-faced and not looking at her, any semblance of humanity or kindness erased—standing next to his lawyer was tough. Linda did a good job.

His lawyer made Beth want to throw up. Half the things he said were lies. The judge made a ruling that took Beth's breath away. How was she going to manage on what Adam was going to pay her? She walked out of the courtroom confused by the result and hurt and furious at Adam.

And that was the beginning of a nine-month slog.

THE DIFFERENT DIVORCES

By now the message should be clear that divorce the old-fashioned way—the currently conventional way—is a draining, destructive process. Here, again, we are speaking of the *legal* divorce. There are many different kinds of divorce. The *psychological divorce* is the process one or both people experience when they realize that the relationship has come to the point that they can no longer stay together. The *social divorce* describes the transition from presenting oneself to your world as part of a couple, part of an entity, to being a single, unattached individual. The *psychic divorce* usually lasts years and tracks the healing and one's emergence as being unmarried, competent, and feeling okay again. For one or both people, this can be a long, many-stepped climb. Then there is the *legal divorce*. This is the process of formally, *legally* severing the marital bond, as well as figuring out what to do with whatever assets and debts have been taken on; providing for support of a spouse and the children; and creating a co-parenting plan.

These elements of the legal divorce *must* eventually be worked out. In order to get married, you just need a certificate. To get divorced, you have to go to court. The difference, of course, is that in divorce there are many issues that people might not agree upon. When there are conflicting interests in our society, which can't get worked out by the people themselves, the courts are the institution we turn to. That, as we have seen, can be quite unfortunate for divorcing people…but there it is. The professionals who guide you through this process are lawyers and judges. These people, as well-meaning and supportive as they might be, are doomed to frustrate, frighten, and ultimately disappoint you. Why would that be?

It's because of *The Seven Cardinal Rules of Legal Divorce*.

RULE NO. 1
LAWYERS ARE TRAINED TO MAKE A
BAD SITUATION WORSE

Sit with a roomful of law students in 2017 and ask them what the lawyer's highest responsibility to a client is, and they would likely say, "Zealous representation." The law students of 1960, 1980, 2010, and all the years in-between, and beyond would say the same. Where does this idea come from...this idea that seems embedded in the lawyer's psyche?

THE BIRTH OF THE "ZEALOUS ADVOCATE"

Because our law comes from England, this is a good place to start in order to understand this rule. Let's travel back to the early nineteenth century.

King George III had much greater headaches after he lost the American colonies in their revolution. The biggest one in his later years was his son, the future King George IV. Having lived a breathtakingly profligate lifestyle, the son George entered his early manhood with debts exceeding $70,000,000 in today's currency. He was both foppish and unpleasant. Finally a match was made with Caroline of Brunswick. It had been agreed that after this regal marriage, the king would persuade Parliament to pay off his son's entire debt.

Caroline was a high-spirited young woman who was positively thrilled at the prospect of becoming Queen of England someday. Those who counseled Caroline before her first voyage to England to meet her future husband advised that her habit of *not* washing herself, or her clothing and covering these habits with considerable powders and perfumes, would not be to her advantage. However, she was stubborn, and George would get his new bride in all of her lusty and rank glory. When she first met the young prince, he immediately turned away from her and demanded a healthy glass of brandy.

Things did not improve. George drank for three days before the royal wedding and had to be carried down the aisle by two attendants. Caroline wrote to a friend afterward, "Judge what it was to have a drunken husband on one's wedding day who passed the greatest part of his bridal night under the grate, where he fell and where I left him."

Relations between husband and wife were chilly, at best, and they spent very little time in each other's company. Caroline took to frequent entertaining, thinking nothing of drinking to excess and dancing with various men, her dress shifting and slipping to expose almost all of her body. After many years of this scandalous estrangement, George finally could stand this no longer, and he sent her away to Italy. While there, Caroline continued her escapades and even took up with a handsome thirty-one-year-old Italian stud from an affluent family.

The long-awaited day finally arrived. King George III died. His son was to ascend to the throne as King George IV, but he did *not* want Caroline to be his Queen. He took the almost unheard-of step of having a bill brought before Parliament seeking a divorce from Caroline, on the grounds of her adulterous Italian relationship. Caroline, upon hearing of this aggressive move on George's part, retained the most accomplished lawyer of the age, Lord Henry Brougham (pronounced "Brome") to defend her. (After all, she had put up with quite a lot of indignities from her husband only so that she could be rewarded some day with a crown. She would not allow him to take this away from her.)

The action in Parliament had deep political undertones that coursed through English society. The populace was fed up with the rule of the Georges, the father having been mad during the end of his reign and the son being a spoiled, self-indulgent buffoon. Both ignored the needs of the people. Many saw Caroline as "the injured Queen," and a good number in the military were said to be siding with her. Civil unrest was a certain threat to the kingdom if the divorce proceeded.

Meanwhile, Caroline's lawyer knew that there had long been a whispered fact about George's youth—that he had married, for love, a young Catholic woman and had never formally divorced her. Lord Brougham let it be known that if George insisted on pursuing his divorce action, *he* would raise the prior marriage to a Catholic and his probable current bigamy. This could well force George to abdicate. The country was astir. Many criticized Brougham for threatening to up the ante in this affair to such a degree as might blow the country apart. Civil War was even being spoken of. To these pleas for caution, Brougham made a statement about a lawyer's duty that rings down to this day, almost 200 years later:

An advocate in the discharge of his duty, knows but one person in all the world, and that person is his client. To save the client by all means and expedients, and at all hazards and costs to other persons...is his first and only duty; and in performing this duty he must not regard the alarm, the torments the destruction which he may bring upon others. Separating the duty of a patriot from that of an advocate, he must go on reckless of consequences, though it should be his unhappy fate to involve his country in confusion.

With the streets roiling, George withdrew his bill of divorcement. However, he physically had Caroline barred from his coronation. Witnesses describe her pounding on the locked castle door, weeping, crying out, "Let me pass. I am your Queen. I am Queen of Britain." She remained barred, and this last gesture of her husband finally broke her. In less than a month, she was dead.

Brougham's declaration crossed the Atlantic and landed on generally willing ears in this country. The isolated objection could be heard, with one judge writing, "It is a popular, but gross mistake, to suppose that a lawyer owes no fidelity to anyone except his client." Still, this was the dominant view of a lawyer's obligation. In 1908, the American Bar Association Ethical Canons required lawyers to represent their clients "zealously within the bounds of the law." Take a moment and consider the word "zealot." That's an awfully intense image, I think you would agree.

Now, you would also admit, I am sure, that if you were ever arrested and charged with a crime, or found your financial security and reputation at risk if someone sued you, no less than the most aggressive attorney you could find, and afford, would do. This lawyer would have to worry *only* about you and your interests. Rest assured that such a person will not be hard to find. These lawyers abound in every community, and they project that commitment very clearly on their websites.

The basic idea supporting this is deceptively simple. If *I* have an aggressive lawyer looking out only for my interests and *you* have an aggressive lawyer looking out only for your interests, then truth will out and justice will be done. When challenged, advocates of this ethical approach might say, "Who am I (as a lawyer) to judge the rightness or wrongness of the other side? That is for the person in robes to decide. If I care about the other side, I will not be giving my all to my client."

This standard way of law-think creates an extremely aggressive and unsettling environment for the non-lawyer participants. This might be one thing for the CEOs of corporations suing over patents, but it is something else altogether if you are getting divorced.

It all starts for young lawyers on their first day of law school. Young men and women from the widest array of backgrounds and interests enter a thought factory that in three years punches out people who have learned to "think like a lawyer." That's the stated goal of law school. Ask most professors who try to instill this approach to understanding and solving problems, and they'll justify their approach thus: Personal values muddy the water and lead to soft thinking. Crisp analysis, not diverted by human emotional concerns, is the cleanest and most effective method of problem-solving and decision-making.

The same is true of today's lawyers who are faced with the many intellectually challenging issues presented by their divorcing clients.

Should the husband who has said for years that he hates his job (and was making plans to transition) be able to change careers at a much-reduced salary when his unemployed wife leaves him? What if they have two kids?

If the wife owned a summer cabin that had been in her family for years when they got married, and it triples in value during the ten-year marriage, is that additional value something that they'll split or is it all hers? Does it matter if the husband spent hundreds of hours over the years doing maintenance?

After a twenty-five-year marriage, should the wife get any part of the husband's inheritance if she was close to her in-laws? Does it matter if she visited her mother-in-law frequently during her last illness? Or if the wife has a successful career? Or if she has been a stay-at-home mom with no employment history, and they don't have any joint, marital assets to speak of?

A husband had married the mother of two kids (two and four years old). Their father is completely uninvolved in their lives, but never consented to the stepdad adopting them, and the mother's new husband was essentially their father for the next dozen years. When that marriage ends, should the husband be permitted any rights to custody or visitation with his stepchildren?

If the husband is a successful lawyer and, three years into the marriage, the wife develops fast-progressing MS, how long should he be expected to provide her support if they divorce after five years? After ten years? Does it matter whether it is a first marriage and they are in their twenties or a later marriage and they are in their fifties?

Questions like these occupy lawyers and judges repeatedly, every day, all over the country. The adversarial training of lawyers, from their earliest days, causes them to view the "opposing party" in a negative light. It is their job to portray that person in an unsympathetic way. Their job, after all, is to "win." Raoul Felder is one of the most successful divorce lawyers in our history. His Manhattan office has handled dozens of high-profile divorces over the years. Some time ago he described his role this way:

> I am tough because I assume the lawyer who opposes me will also be tough. I will do anything within the law and the ethics of my profession to deserve the confidence placed in me.... It is not my intention to stand in judgment. I am not a moralist or a minister, a priest, or a rabbi. As a lawyer, I am a technician, a how-to man.... When I take a case, I am not concerned with whether my client is right or wrong. As far as I am concerned, a client is always right. I may refuse to represent him for other reasons...but not because I think he's in the wrong. To stand in judgment is too great a luxury.[4]

While Felder is in the business of celebrity divorce, where management of the press and dividing multimillion dollar estates is the norm, his expression of professional philosophy applies equally to lawyers who handle the divorces of Donald Trump's gardener and Tom Cruise's kids' fourth-grade teacher, as well. This combination of single-pointed focus on the interests of the client only, and the push to depersonalize the struggles of the "opposing" individuals, is tough on the people sucked into that system. Add to this the searing emotional challenges of divorce (as we will see later), and, well, lawyers are trained to make a bad situation worse.

RULE NO. 2
JUDGES DO NOT DISPENSE JUSTICE

Back in the 1980s, there was this widely respected and accomplished family lawyer from Sausalito, California, named Stephen Adams. He was considered by many to be *the* expert in California divorce law. Annually, he would go around the state and lecture in hotel ballrooms packed with family lawyers, reviewing the past year's developments. I came away from my first such conference with two distinct impressions: One, there were a lot of family lawyers who were committed to being at the top of their craft. Two, the guy was absolutely brilliant. Adams told this story about his days in practice:

Clients would often arrive for their first meeting with him filled with righteousness. They felt wronged and **they…wanted…justice**! Adams suggested to these people that they ought to go down to the courthouse and sit in on a morning's worth of family law hearings. He told them it would help orient them and, when he had to take them into court soon, they'd be more comfortable with the proceedings.

What he didn't tell them was that he also wanted them to see how courts operated. He wanted them to observe judges slashing, burning, and pillaging the cases before them. He wanted his clients to see the reactions of litigants after a judge's ruling. After the experience, he would nail them with the message, "Forget your *day in court.*"

The days of judges having the chance to contemplate the cause before them and render *Solomonic Justice* are long gone, if they ever existed in the first place. Judges are overworked "deciders." With the explosion of lawyers over the past decades has come the accompanying huge increase in legal cases. The no-fault divorce revolution of the 1970s put further pressure on family law judges' calendars. The men and women in robes hear thousands of requests for temporary orders in divorce cases each year. Managing a caseload becomes a valued skill. Judges are administrators as much as contemplators, perhaps even more so.

Divorce amplifies this problem, because of the volume of people who come before the court not represented by lawyers. A lot more people get divorced than have auto accidents or bring other kinds of lawsuits. Getting divorced doesn't mean you have money. In fact, one reason people get divorced is financial stress. Many thousands of couples get divorced in this country every year who can't afford lawyers. This doesn't mean they know how to navigate the court system, though. Hardly any non-lawyers know what forms to use, what court deadlines are, or what constitutes the kind of proof that deciders sitting on their benches need in order to come down on one side or the other. Legal proceedings are technical, and many is the poor soul who has gotten lost in the maze. Judges and court commissioners spend countless hours explaining things to unrepresented citizens. With the already high caseloads, this allows even less time to devote to individual matters. How do judges cope?

Well, for one thing, when you see the same kind of problems and arguments over and over, day after day, for months and years, you cannot help but develop your own shorthand. Cases begin to fit into certain boxes in your head. Judges are human beings, and attempts to train bias out of their brains is a daunting task. Try as they might, judges who are careful to guard against the most obvious biases cannot escape their own life experience. As noted by one New Mexico family law judge,[5]

> Too few judges and lawyers have examined their personal beliefs, attitudes, and expectations about family matters in any depth, and that leaves them vulnerable to becoming emotionally entangled in divorce and custody cases, sometimes quite unconsciously....What does reach their conscious awareness is that they are extremely uncomfortable, but they haven't the skills to reflect on their discomfort through introspection. In short, family law has a propensity to diminish objectivity and blur boundaries for judges and lawyers and thus cause emotional overload.

Excellent examples of bias based on personal experience can be found as high as the country's Supreme Court. Take Justice Antonin Scalia, for example. Scalia, a devout Catholic, was born in 1937. His generation and personal background were certainly not conducive to appreciating any benefits to be had from mental health counseling. I think it is safe to say that Justice Scalia never sat across from a therapist when he was troubled. Since he was always gleefully unabashed in expression of his beliefs, it is not surprising that his own bias leaked out in an opinion he wrote in 1996 about therapy.

The question was whether there was a therapist-patient privilege, which prevented a social worker from having to testify in Federal Court about a client's disclosures to her in their sessions. The court's opinion said that such protection did exist, but Scalia dissented, saying no such privilege should apply in Federal Courts (despite the fact that every state had such protections in their own courts). In a revealing passage, Justice Scalia noted,[6]

> *When is it, one must wonder, that the psychotherapist came to play such an indispensable role in the maintenance of the citizenry's mental health? For most of history, men and women have worked out their difficulties by talking to (among others), parents, siblings, best friends and bartenders—none of whom was awarded a privilege against testifying in court. Ask the average citizen: Would your mental health be more significantly impaired by preventing you from seeing a psychotherapist, or by preventing you from getting advice from your mom? I have little doubt what the answer would be. Yet there is no mother child privilege.*

Yes, I know what you're thinking: "Why *isn't* there a bartender-customer privilege?" That is a discussion for another day. Seriously, though, it is hard to read the above passage and not be struck by Antonin Scalia's (1) unfamiliarity with the counseling relationship and its value, and, (2) his resultant bias.

Divorce judges are no less prone to their own impressions gained from life experience. How can a judge who is a divorced single mother, having raised her children without the help of her absent ex-husband, not be impacted in her decision-making? Is she going to be sympathetic to the stay-at-home mother who claims that she needs support for years because she has no job skills? Do family court judges have their own ideas about whether an unskilled stay-at-home *father* would be entitled to the same amount of alimony for the same length of time as a mom in the same situation? Is it okay to leave children alone at home for three hours when they are twelve? How about ten? Is it harmful for a child to be raised by a gay or lesbian couple? In almost every state, "fault" cannot be taken into consideration when deciding how marital property is to be divided. Even if this is the law, might the judge still be impacted by the fact that a man leaves his wife of forty years for a younger woman? What if the judge, a woman, had lost her husband in a similarly humiliating manner? What if that younger woman then divorces the older man?

I just can't pass up the opportunity to share one of the greatest examples of gender bias that ever ended up in a trial transcript. As you will see, the moral of this story is, "If you are a judge and there is a court reporter taking down everything you say, *don't think out loud!*"

In the early 1990s, there was a divorce trial before an Orange County, California, judge. The separating spouses were arguing over the validity of a premarital contract. The husband was older and wealthy. The woman was young and attractive. She moved into his home and later they were married. Both husband and wife said it was the *other's* idea to get married. In deciding that it could not have been the husband's idea to marry a younger woman who was living with him (and noting that he didn't look like John Wayne and "even if we take 17 years off him, I don't think he looks like Adonis"), the judge proceeded to muse on the record,

> *I cannot accept the fact that, as she said, he was the one that proposed marriage to her. That would be the last thing that would be on his mind. And why, in heaven's name, do you buy the cow when you get the milk free, as we used to say. And, so, he's getting the milk free. And [she] is living with him in his home.*
>
> *And the impetus for marriage must be coming from her side, because there's nothing [he] is going to get out of it. Marriage is a drag on the market. It's a deprivation of his freedom. He's got everything that he would want out of a relationship with none of the obligations.*[7]

This example, while almost comically tone-deaf and extreme, highlights a lower-grade, more pervasive worry. Many is the lawyer who has put on a solid case only to get a ruling that leaves them shaking their heads. A judge might like or despise someone, and nobody would know. *The judge might not even know*. For all their education, training, and care in their thinking, judges don't exactly get much opportunity for self-exploration. "Counter-transference," which is the unconscious, biased reaction of a therapist to a client (be it attraction or repulsion) is only lightly touched on in a handful of client counseling classes in law school. It is, as far as I know, non-existent in judicial training.

There is another element of the judicial mindset we might call "The George W. Bush Effect." Most recall his statement, "I'm the decider." While expressed in his usually inelegant fashion, he spoke a real truth. There are people whose jobs are to decide. It is an executive function as essential to heads of businesses as it is to heads of state. Judges are professional deciders. In fact, if you have difficulty making decisions—if you are an "on the one hand…but on the other hand" person—being a judge is not for you. In order to be an effective decider, you will not belabor the decision you have made. It's "make the call and then move on to the next one." Judges are almost always done considering a question once they have made a decision. That is why they become extremely impatient with people who want to keep up the argument. They are done. The door is closed. Right or wrong, it is time to move on. Of course, once the decision is made, to keep one's balance, you can't worry about whether or not the decision was wrong.

Finally, there is *no way* any judge can know you or the intricacies of your situation as well as you do. Pauline Tesler, a highly respected lawyer and a trainer out of the San Francisco Bay Area, once illustrated the following problem in this way (as I recall it now many years later): As we walk through this, I invite you to find a regular piece of 8 ½ x 11 paper. Now imagine you are a divorcing spouse and that paper contains all the intricacies of your situation—what drives you and what worries you, the big themes and little facts, and, most importantly, the history of your marriage and how it broke down. *Now fold the paper in half*. This is the amount of information you can transmit to your lawyer about your situation. *Now fold the paper in half again*. This is the amount of information the lawyer takes in as worthy of note in representing you. *Now fold the paper in half again.* This is the amount of information the lawyer believes is relevant to a court and will be put in the court papers. *Now fold the paper in half again.* This is the amount of information that the judge registers as important when reading the paperwork. *Now fold it in half again.* This is the information the judge says she bases her decision on.

Now compare the full paper and the folded paper. Here, I'll help you:

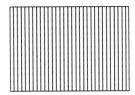

A.   Your Story

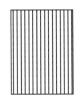

B. What You Tell Your
Lawyer

C. What Your Lawyer
Hears

D. What Goes In
the Lawyer's Papers

E. What the Judge
Listens to

F. The Judge's
Reasoning for the
Decision

Now compare:

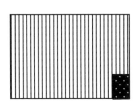

This is why you don't want a judge to decide your divorce case if you can avoid it.

<u>**RULE NO. 3**</u>
THE DICKENS RULE:
LEGAL DIVORCE COMES AT THE WORST TIME
AND THE BEST TIME

This is how Charles Dickens begins his classic, *A Tale of Two Cities*: "It was the best of times, it was the worst of times...." Such can be said for the timing of the legal divorce.

As for the worst time—people will usually come face to face with legal divorce and the decisions that have to be made very early in the psychological divorce process. Almost without exception, we are overwhelmed by the strongest feelings. Anger or grief might predominate. It is common that fear, shame, confusion, and a pressing need to blame grab hold of the divorcing spouse. What a terrible mindset to struggle with while you must make some of the biggest decisions of your life. Make no mistake, the decisions that must be made in divorce will have enormous consequences for the rest of one's days. To make these decisions thoughtfully, we need to be able to project ourselves years into the future and understand how the agreements we make now will be impacting us then. Goodness, there are a myriad of moving parts to any divorce resolution. Few things in our lives will call upon our utmost left brain capacity. Do I want to stay in the family home? Can I afford it? Do I want to have cash or retirement (if it has to be one or the other)? What kind of residential schedule is best for the kids, and how do I assess that without confusing my best interests with theirs? What kind of plans should I make (*can* I make) for their education? I've been out of the working world raising our kids for twelve years; how am I going to take care of myself and my kids now? How will my life look in five years? Fifteen years? Will I want to move with the children? Is that best for them? For me? If we're lucky enough to have a collection of different kinds of assets, which ones would be best for me, given my future plans? Will I need short-term cash, or might non-liquid retirement assets be more appropriate in the long term?

Amidst all this left brain calculation, there is the emotional part of the brain hammering away: "That bastard is already with a new woman!" "She stayed at home and painted her nails while I slaved away, and now she wants half?" "We were going to grow old together like my mom and dad—now what am I going to do? I'm so scared, I haven't slept more than two hours a night in the past month!" "I am such a failure. I'm fifty; my youth is gone—how am I ever going to find someone?" "She's so angry at me—there's no way she's going to let me be with my kids. I have lost my family."

Imagine having to think clearly with *that* kind of noise going on in your head. As we'll see later, the emotional/psychological divorce process can take about two years to work its way through. Your brain is going to be in a much better place to make important decisions then. So legal divorce, which is an early challenge in this lengthy journey, comes at the worst of times.

On the other hand…there is hardly a more disorienting time in your life than your divorce time. It's as if you are floating in space. There is no foundation upon which you can stand. Nothing is reliable anymore. The relationship you have with your soon-to-be-ex is loosey-goosey. "How do I figure out the finances and pay the bills?" "When are the kids with her and when are they with me?" "Who stays in the house while this pig (the legal divorce) is moving through the belly of the snake?" "Fourth of July is coming up—will the kids be with me and my folks this year?"

The insecurity of not knowing is the hardest thing. The anxiety can feel intolerable. Here's where temporary agreements or court orders can be valuable. You have a roadmap. It can be the key to your sanity during this unstable period in your life. It can form a foundation upon which confused, disoriented people may stand. So legal divorce, with its agreements and early court orders, can come at the best of times as well (you might say a "necessary time")…or at least, so says Charles Dickens, divorce lawyer.

RULE NO. 4
LEGAL DIVORCE IS ALL ABOUT LOSS

When you are married, your house is yours. It's your spouse's too…but it's still yours. You get your kids all the time when they are home, even if they are off to the zoo with the other parent. Your life and family and just about everything you have is both of yours. There's a legal term for this. It's called an "undivided interest." It's a natural state of mind as well.

Then the divorce occurs, and *legal* divorce is all about dividing everything up. Time with the kids, property and debts, income. Suddenly something you felt you owned *all of,* you're only going to get *part* of. This is particularly distressing for anyone who felt that they worked hard during the marriage to earn that thing and now they're only going to get part of it. Boy, try telling a guy who's been working at a job he doesn't like for years earning a good pension, that it's not *his* pension, but a *marital* pension that his wife gets part of. Be sure to duck. He might not be happy with that reality.

Divorce lawyers and judges make one important mistake about "things." They think that it is idiotic folly to fight over a toaster. While running up hundreds of dollars in fees to fight over items worth a fraction of that amount seems nuts, that's only because they are seeing with their heads, not their hearts. Logically, there is no reason to struggle over seemingly replaceable things. Emotionally, however, there are people who have such a vulnerability to loss in their lives that giving up certain things feels like a death. (Sure, there are people who demand certain things as part of a power play or effort to spite the other, who does invest meaning in the object. That happens plenty, but to what end? To punish or cause pain to your soon-to-be ex? If that is still the motivating force behind divorce decisions, you will not end up with good decisions. Again, the post-divorce years will be spent healing from unnecessary divorce-created wounds, rather than devoting psychic energy to creating and pursuing one's life course. The natural recovery process will be slowed to a crawl with such diversion of inner resources. Coming out the other end will take many months and, for a great number, many years.)

Things absorb and reflect our memories, just as do songs or movies or photographs. I've got an attachment to our Cuisinart, for the memories of great dinner parties we have had over the years. Cuisinart means friends (and that nasty cut on my finger once). There's this vibrantly colored porcupine made out of wood we've got, with little painted toothpicks as quills. It's kind of cute, but it wouldn't garner more than a buck or two at a garage sale. The reason I love it is that it reminds me of the wonderful weekend we spent at the Ashland, Oregon, Shakespeare Festival, where we bought it years ago. I look at the thing and can conjure up reading *The Merry Wives of Windsor* so I could understand the play when we saw it there, and then seeing the play itself. The people in Ashland were completely set up for tourists during the summer, and it's hard to imagine a more welcoming place. The B&B was a half-hour walk out of downtown, and the evenings were warm and gorgeous. I was deeply in love that weekend.

That's what my porcupine says to me.

That's not to mention the mundane stuff. The pots and pans, beds and bureaus, couches, flat screens, towels and sheets, kids' stuff—the list goes on and on. She'll get the kids' bedroom furniture, so he's got to replace that. She's got to buy a new TV. If they've got to sell the house, there won't be room for the trampoline in the new places. The kids will definitely not be happy with that. Losing a pet to the other person is a heartbreak. The house…the house is *huge*. If it has to be sold, the adults and kids see this big chunk of their lives fly away. If Mom stays in the house, Dad will be torn, and heartsick, because now he will be "visiting" what used to his home.

True, loss is part of the whole divorce process, not just limited to the *legal* divorce. However, the professionals who assist people with this process are society's left brain poster children—the judges and lawyers. The loss that comes with dividing up "stuff" might often seem trivial and beside the point to them.

What everyone *does* get is that this family's lifestyle will nosedive (for all but the wealthy). Vacations, new clothes, eating out, subscription TV services, church or other charitable donations, a new computer, going to ball games or concerts, entertaining at home, housekeepers/gardeners, camp for the kid—these and many more things will be cut back or eliminated. When a sudden emergency expense arises—car repair, hot water heater replacement, or a medical procedure—the financial stresses can be acute. The financial divorce is a central part of the legal divorce—and it is all about loss. This is something the legal divorce forces us to face.

<u>RULE NO. 5</u>
BOTH PEOPLE COME AWAY FEELING THEY
GOT SCREWED AND THEIR PARTNER DIDN'T

When I was practicing law, many was the time that a client would come into my office and tell their story, and my first impressions was, "This is a loser. If they go to court, they are going to get clobbered." Then, I would think about their position and the reasons they said or did what they described, and I began to appreciate the kernel of righteousness in their position. Since there are almost always two sides to every story (at least), it isn't hard to climb on an individual's bandwagon. (By the way, this is why lawyers are not hypocrites for making one argument one day and the opposite argument the next.) Dive ever more deeply into one person's side of an argument and you come to *believe*. There is hardly a person who makes their pitch to a decision-maker in an adversarial legal proceeding who doesn't truly, deeply, wholeheartedly *believe* in what they are saying. The problem with arguing your position in front of a judge is that she will make a decision in favor of one person or the other. Sometimes she will give one person a bit and the other a bit, but, much more frequently, one person will win and the other will lose.

How does the person—who had come to believe completely, utterly, in the rightness (the *righteousness)* of their position—who hears a negative ruling from the bench feel? "Unfair," "stupid," or "prejudiced" is the natural reaction. Almost never is it, "Oh…I thought I was right but maybe I wasn't." This is experienced by the lawyer as well, as they have shifted over time from seeing their client's position as a "loser" (in cases when that *is* their initial hit), to convincing themselves that they should win. If they started out thinking they had a winner, the shock of loss is more acute, the task of explaining to the client more challenging.

The same dynamic dogs the individual who must wrestle with settling their case. It is a basic tenet of psychology, as we have seen, that people will be more sensitive to loss than gain. When people settle their case, it is almost axiomatic that the next morning, they will be plagued with doubt and resentment about the things *they gave up*. In forty years of practicing law, I almost never heard a client say, "I know I gave up some things, but I am satisfied with what I got." Instead, there is a preoccupation with what was given up—what was lost. Time and again, this is the outcome from settlement in an adversarial divorce process. *Each* person does it, so there is scant satisfaction on either side, as both feel they got screwed by the outcome and the other didn't.

I had a colleague who decided to abandon the practice of adversarial divorce and pursue collaborative law when she took a parenting case in which her client had mental health and alcohol issues. She was able to persuade him to get counseling and enter rehab. The mother of his three children had been the primary caretaker, and she had initially wanted to limit his time with the children to a couple of hours on a weekend day, to be supervised for their safety. He worked hard in therapy, started a course of antidepressant medication, and, when the court finally made its decision, he had been clean and sober for six months. As he straightened out his life, he came to believe he should have equal residential time, and my colleague told him that he wasn't likely to achieve that goal. She put an enormous amount of time, energy, and emotional investment into his case. The judge gave him much more unsupervised residential time than he had any hope of achieving at the start of the case, but when they left the courtroom, he turned to my colleague and said, "You and that judge didn't do me any favors." While a dramatic example, this does fairly reflect the natural reactions people have when faced with the challenges of an adversarial divorce. I have little doubt, as well, that the mom in that case was outraged that the man she had convinced herself was alcoholic and irresponsible received unsupervised time with her children.

Years ago, when considering a transition from personal injury to family law, I had a number of "informational interviews" with divorce lawyers. I asked them about the expressions of appreciation they received from their clients and was struck by the almost universal experience of being cut off by their clients after the litigation dust had settled. I remember one advising me pointedly, "Your clients won't want to even think of you when the case is done, as you represent the most painful experience in their lives."

_____

RULE NO. 6
LEGAL DIVORCE IS EXPENSIVE

If you decide to litigate your divorce, you're going to have to open your wallet and harden your heart. That university education for your kids will now be going to your lawyer's children. That's not because lawyers are slimy or greedy (well, they *could be*, but that's rare). The whole system is set up to suck the change from your pockets like an efficient vacuum.

We can start with the attorneys. There was a time, back in the foggy mists of history—before the 1960s—where lawyers would charge for the job. Hourly billing is a relatively new development in the big picture. Lawyers' hourly rates are quite high. Paralegals, who do a lot of the legwork in these cases, charge a lot per hour, too—not as much as the lawyers by a long shot, but still a lot. In decent-sized cities, experienced divorce lawyers charge anywhere between $300 and $500 per hour. Paralegals might be in the range of $100 to $175, or more, per hour. These fees can multiply quickly. When the lawyer and paralegal discuss strategy for an hour, the bill will reflect the lawyer's $300 charge *and* the paralegal's $150 charge. An hour of professional service, then, will cost you $450.

Unlike litigation between Microsoft and Apple, where each has its own budget and source for paying lawyers, divorce attorneys' fees come out of one coffer: It is the marital estate that will pay these fees. The savings account or other liquid asset will often be accessed for payment of these professional fees. If the couple can't agree on early, pressing matters, they will have to go to court and fight over temporary orders to establish some status quo until trial or settlement. Let's say preparing all the paperwork and appearing in court will take 5 hours of a lawyer's time and 20 hours of a paralegal's time. At $300 and $125 per hour, that's $1,500 and $2,500, for a total of $4,000. Now double that, because there are two sides billing out at that level, and we're talking $8,000 for just the beginning of the case—and plenty of these early court appearances cost twice as much as that, or more. It is not unheard of for litigated divorces, even without trials, to cost each side more than $25,000—that's $50,000 from the same pot of resources (and colleagues who have reviewed this manuscript say this figure might even be low).

Another problem about costs arises when you decide to hire a lawyer in a law firm, rather than a sole practitioner or a small, two- or three-person firm. Young lawyers have a primary obligation to their employer, and that is to have billable hours. Almost every firm of even middling size requires their junior lawyers to meet a certain minimum of billable hours per month. That's how you get ahead in the firm. In the macho world of litigation, finding a way to bill an average of ten hours per day is a sign of diligence. You are partner material! Note that the incentive isn't to perform legal services as economically as possible. It is quite the opposite. The rationale for this enormous emphasis on putting in billable hours is that it takes time to be prepared and to know a case thoroughly. This is what you've got to do to zealously represent the interests of your client. While that is certainly true, it's not cheap.

To be sure, while it is impressive to walk into a lawyer's office and gaze out at a magnificent vista (Seattle, where I live, boasts breathtaking views of Mt. Rainier out the wall of plate glass windows in firm conference rooms), these views don't come cheap. Magnificent art and tasteful design are also both impressive and pricey. You're paying for that overhead.

It's not just the lawyers you'll be paying for if you go to the mat. Parenting evaluations can be extremely expensive. In some places, there is a neutral parenting evaluator whose work is scrutinized by experts for each side, resulting in a total cost that can reach into the high four-figures or beyond. Courts are jammed and cases can be delayed and bounced around from judge to judge. In order to get things resolved in a decently quick way, people often hire arbitrators to act as private judges. These people are often retired judges, and they don't come cheap. There can be a bunch of other professionals and experts that people might need if they are going to gird for this battle. You could find yourself retaining real estate appraisers, business valuation experts, vocational counselors, psychologists, substance abuse experts, tax experts, certified divorce financial analysts (CDFAs), or CPAs to value pensions.

If you are going to litigate your divorce and fight for what you are "entitled to," it will have to come at a price. What you *don't* want is someone working for you who is slipshod and distracted by too many clients and obligations. Care takes time. Time costs money. Litigation is expensive.

<u>RULE NO. 7</u>
DIVORCE LAWYERS AND CLIENTS SPEAK DIFFERENT LANGUAGES

About thirty years ago, a couple of professors, Austin Sarat and William Felstiner, decided they wanted to study how divorce lawyers interacted with their clients. They were able to convince a number of lawyers to allow them to sit in on attorney-client meetings in cases, from the first interview to the final result. In small-to-medium sized firms in California and Massachusetts, they sat in on 115 attorney-client meetings and interviewed everyone involved at different points in the process. Their 1995 book *Divorce Lawyers and Their Clients* is fascinating reading for anyone interested in how these people speak to each other *and* hear each other.

Their observations are as accurate now as they were when this book was written.

Noting the challenge for clients, they poignantly observed:

> *Dealing with a divorce lawyer means having to expose the most intimate details of one's personal and financial life to a stranger. It means having to trust the lawyer's commitment and loyalty at a time when a far stronger set of commitments and loyalties have proven untrustworthy.*

This trust is sorely tested, because lawyers and their clients are not speaking the same language and strongly feel that different things are important.

What is important to the client is sorting out the feelings of guilt, betrayal, and blame that almost always accompany the end of a marriage. Lawyers, though, are living in another world. In one excellent description of lawyers' thinking, it was observed:

> *Think for a moment about a lawyer's ability to listen. Like a falcon that scours the ground from dizzying heights, spots something moving and instantly determines its*

mealworthiness, a lawyer scans the environment for information, captures it, analyzes it and uses it to build a case to solve the problem at hand.[8]

Lawyers have a special filter fitted over their brains when dealing with clients. Only those things that are legally relevant are worth spending time on. While no-fault divorce *did* lessen the destructive drama of the legal part of splitting up, it suddenly made irrelevant the *things that are most relevant to many clients.* While a person might complain loud and long about how their spouse is acting like a jerk, if it doesn't help to achieve some result in the legal case, it's just noise to the lawyer.

There are also serious limitations in the kind of outcome, or "relief," that the law can provide in legal divorce. Clients want "justice." Yet, justice is not a realistic goal in divorce litigation, because lawyers know it is simply not attainable. The purpose of the whole process is seen differently by the two major actors in the drama.

The two people will talk over and under each other, never quite connecting:

> *The client's life at work, and with friends or parents, is largely ignored. Unless they are trying to explain or predict spousal behavior that is directly relevant to the divorce process, lawyers rarely even inquire about the client's social world. Lawyers are, however, continually confronted by clients who want to discuss the causes of marriage failure and the content of relations with their spouse during the divorce, as well as matters occurring at work or with friends.... Where the issue is marriage failure, lawyers retreat in silence and at the first opportunity change the subject, often quite abruptly.*

The *legal divorce* is focused on ending the individuals' status as married persons and to provide for their future financial relationship (in terms of dividing assets and liabilities and resolving alimony concerns) and the co-parenting relationship. The other elements of their divorce—how they recover from this deeply personal loss; figuring out what friends will stay with which partner; managing the emotional blow of a spouse's new romantic relationship (either before or after the divorce); facing the sense of failure that haunts many divorcing people—unfold during and after the conclusion of the legal divorce process. The inordinate stresses of the adversarial legal divorce process mesh with the natural psychological stresses of divorcing. Yet they are different, and divorcing individuals will be managing their "divorce recovery process" long after their lawyers and the courthouse are fading to dots in their rearview mirrors.

THINKING ABOUT *THINKING* LAWYERS

Larry Richards had been a lawyer for a number of years and decided to shift careers and earn a PhD in psychology. He came up with a clever idea for his dissertation—combining his two interests. He had become well versed in the popular personality sorter, the Myers-Briggs Type Indicator, and he focused his study on lawyers and psychological type.

Back in the early 1940s, Katharine Briggs and her daughter, Isabel Briggs Myers, put together a "forced choice" personality sorter that was based in part on the book *Psychological Types* by Carl Jung and in part on their own observations of family and friends. There were a bit over 100 items, which asked people to choose which statement or description, between two choices, most fit them. Examples are: "Do you consider yourself to be (a) more of a spontaneous person or (b) more of an organized person?" and, "Do you find being around a lot of people (a) gives you more energy or (b) is often 'draining'?"

There are four sets of preferences that arise from these answers. (Note, there is a lot that can be said about each of these four different categories, and I am only touching upon single elements to illustrate what I want to say about lawyers.)

The first is Extraversion/Introversion. Generally speaking, do you tend to direct your life energy outward, having a broader group of friends and connections while processing your thoughts out in the world? If so, you are a Myers-Briggs *Extravert*. By contrast, is your focus inward, tending to be more reserved, with fewer, deeper, connections, speaking only after you have thought through what it is you want to share? You would, then, prefer *Introversion*.

The next category describes how we take in information about the world and process that information. *Sensing* types are drawn to that which is experienced through the five senses. Reality is trusted as it is experienced. If an approach has worked before, it is preferred over a new, untried idea. Problems are thought through sequentially and details are important. *Intuitive* types prefer to experience the world through the *connections* and *patterns* they perceive through their senses. The interesting, the novel, and creative are fascinating, and these people are drawn to future possibilities. They skip details in preference to the big picture. *Sensors* are natural reality-testers and *Intuitives* are the drivers toward innovation. Each needs the other's influence.

The next category describes how we make decisions about the information we absorb. *Thinking* types make decisions through their logical reasoning process. These folks can be pretty dispassionate, which is very helpful when others are being thrown off by their own strong emotions. While *Thinkers* have emotions, they are a bit uneasy with feelings and much prefer to make decisions without interference from emotion. *Feeling* types make decisions based upon two important factors: How a decision fits with their deep sense of personal values and how the decision impacts other people. *Feelers* tend to be more empathic and interpersonally warm. They can be thrown off by the absence of appreciation and collegiality in a work or living environment, while this is just not an important factor for the *Thinking* type. Strong *Thinkers* will see the strong *Feeler* as overly soft or mushy while the responding critique leveled at *Thinkers* will be "heartless."

The final category includes the *Judging* types, who prefer things to be organized and operate most comfortably within a structure. These folks are planners and do have a strong idea of the way things *should* be. While others might be better at starting things, the *Judgers* are excellent at seeing things through to completion. In fact, making decisions is one of their strong suits. Having things resolved is a high value for them. In contrast, the *Perceiving* types like to observe. They want to keep their options open and, in fact, have some difficulty making decisions. "Don't fence me in," is their theme song. While organization is a quality much valued in *Judging* types, flexibility is embraced by *Perceivers*.

So back to Larry Richard, who in the early '90s asked the president of the American Bar Association to endorse his study of lawyers using the MBTI. He sent a few thousand of these instruments to practicing lawyers, with the support of the ABA, and received a remarkably high return rate. His analysis of the results formed the basis of a fascinating and deeply insightful cover article in the *ABA Journal*. One of his findings helps explain the disconnect between divorce lawyers and their clients.

While the Thinking/Feeling difference is generally understood to be the most gender related, with roughly 65% of men in our culture preferring *Thinking* and about the same percentage of women preferring *Feeling*, legal education and training throws this distribution out of whack. Some 83% of the male lawyers in Richard's study were *Thinking* types and 65% of the female lawyers were *Thinking* types. Another study of California judges found 85% of the men to be *Thinking* types.

When young people begin law school, their professors consider it a solemn duty to teach them to "think like a lawyer." That's a stock phrase that almost any attorney you speak to will recall from those early days of their career path. What does that mean? Simply that the law school experience drives the Feeling orientation of analysis and decision-making as far from one's consciousness as possible.

Scott Turow, the former lawyer and author of *Presumed Innocent* and other blockbusters, wrote a book years ago describing his experience as a first-year law student. A passage in *One L* perfectly describes this indoctrination and the reaction of those students with more of a Feeling orientation to the analytic method as taught by Professors Morris, Perini and Mann:

> *We all quickly saw that that kind of argument was supposed to be reasoned, consistent, progressive in its logic. Nothing was taken for granted; nothing was proven just because it was strongly felt. All of our teachers tried to impress upon us that you do not sway a judge with emotional declarations of faith. Nicky Morris often derided responses as "sentimental goo," and Perini on more than one occasion quickly dispatched students who tried to argue by asserting*

supposedly irreducible principles.... With relative speed, we all seemed to gain skill in reconciling and justifying our positions.... But to Gina, the process which had brought that kind of change about was frightening and objectionable.

"I don't care if Bertram Mann (the criminal law professor) doesn't want to know how I feel about prostitution," she said that day at lunch. "I feel a lot of things about prostitution, and they have everything to do with the way I think about prostitution. I don't want to become the kind of person who tries to pretend that my feelings have nothing to do with my opinions. It's not bad to feel things."

A study of law students and psychological type from way back in the 1960s revealed that the greatest dropout rate was found in students preferring a *Feeling* orientation. Indeed, the practice of law, with its over-reliance on hard-headed logic and relative dismissal of how its workings affect the hearts and minds of real people who are sucked into its machine, is the perfect representation of a profession of *Thinking* Types. There has been a strong push-back in recent years, as will be described in later chapters.

Yet, while the *legal* divorce is a hugely challenging process, it isn't the only divorce we experience. Numerous studies, and millions of words, have issued forth over the years about the *psychological* divorce. Divorce is a process, rather than a single event. Its impact on our lives spreads out through the ensuing years like ripples from the stone dropped into a pond. Perhaps the greatest significance of the *legal* divorce, and how it is handled, lies in those ripples. They are inevitable—but will they be manageable or large enough to swamp our psyches and our lives? That is the subject of the next chapter.

TAKEAWAYS

- **The legal divorce is only one of the many kinds of divorce processes, with its own rules and coping strategies.**
- **Divorce lawyers are overwhelmingly good people who ply their trade in a process ill-suited to managing the challenges of divorce.**

- It is important to understand your goals at the beginning of a legal divorce. Write them down and, if you have a professional advisor, be they a lawyer or counselor, share these goals. Be open to letting go of those which are unrealistic or unattainable (starting with "justice"). Get help managing the natural grief that arises when you abandon justice, as you understand it, in your legal divorce.

CHAPTER 4

The Psychology of Divorce

Adam

    Adam sat with June after dinner, lingering over his glass of wine, and breathed in the warming spring air coming through the window. He felt content on this gentle evening. They had been married for five years, and he believed they were going to be lifers. His divorce from Beth was seven years gone now, and they had managed to build a decent, though guarded, co-parenting relationship. After six years on her own, Beth had found a guy she seemed happy with. They weren't married, but the kids had told him they were planning on moving in together. They seemed to like this guy, Alex, and that made Adam happy.

    He never figured out what the hell had happened with Beth. It was like she went through a change of life or something. Suddenly out of the blue she said she wanted a divorce. Sure, Adam had reacted strongly for a while, and why not? His world had just cascaded down around his ears. Those first couple of years were wild. As he recalls it:

"First there was Susie. There'd been nothing there before Beth threw me out, regardless of what she thought. I mean, I *liked* her, don't get me wrong, and thought she was fun, but I was married. Even if I was horny, I wasn't going to do anything. I enjoyed flirting around with Susie, but that was it. Then, when the divorce happened, well, it was just like a big green light as far as I was concerned. I'll tell you this— the sex was fantastic. It had been a long time. Trust me on that. Beth went from passionate to pretty much nothing. She didn't seem to like me touching her, and I don't think she once responded to a sexual overture during the last three years of our marriage. We'd have sex maybe once every three months or so. By the last year, even that didn't happen. I've got to admit it, though. Susie was hot and I missed sex—good sex—so much. I loved sex with Susie. Probably not the smartest thing I ever did, and when it ended after six months and word spread around the office and Susie started making noises about harassment, I was forced out of my job. That drove Beth (and her lawyer) crazy for a couple of months. We got nasty letters about irresponsible *this* and taking the house and all my retirement *that*, but it eventually smoothed out when I landed with a competitor, making the same money.

Those were the darkest days. Everyone seemed to be hating me except for my lawyer (and he was being paid to love me!). My daughter didn't want to come visit for nine months. I had been busting my ass for Beth and the kids—and for what? To be thrown out for no reason. We didn't have a perfect marriage. Who does? She seemed to resent me for all the things I liked about myself—hardworking, good with people, steady. I never got drunk, never touched her, or, what do they call it?—"emotionally abused" her in any way. I kept my mouth shut when she'd complain—and then she'd complain about my keeping my mouth shut. I never figured out what she wanted. I did my best and she made me feel like a criminal.

That first year after I left was hell. Every time I talked to Beth, she'd be either angry or depressed. I didn't get it. *She* was the one who asked me for a divorce. Thank God Beth was such a good mom and didn't pitch a fit when I asked to switch weekends sometimes. She kept the house, and I spent two years in a tiny, two-bedroom apartment. I paid my child support and alimony on time every month. I didn't have much extra, so when Beth would ask for some extra money for an activity for the kids, I told her she needed to ask her folks because I was tapped out. She'd make cracks about my trips to Park City or Maui, and I know it filtered down to the kids because they'd be sullen a lot of times when they were with me.

Well, I'm not one to whine and I have always landed on my feet. I met June my first month of dating online. She'd been divorced for five years and shares her son with her ex 50/50. I made sure Lilly and Jason gave her a thumbs-up. Her son Nick's a good kid and we get along okay. I wish Beth well, I really do. But I'm much happier with June. She's a better fit for me, and when Nick graduates from high school later this year, I look forward to more her and me time. She travels a lot for her job, too, so it gives me a lot of opportunity to miss her."

THE HARDEST BLOW
~ DIVORCE AS AN "ATTACHMENT INJURY" ~

In the 1960s, Thomas Holmes and Richard Rahe, a couple of sociologists, were curious about how stress might heighten the risk of illness. So, they did what sociologists do—they designed a research project. They went into hospitals and asked 5,000 sick people to list what events they had experienced in the past year. The responses helped them generate a collection of 43 stressful life events that patients had experienced. This list ranged from the hammer blows of death of a spouse or serving time in prison, to the less intense, but still measuring on the stress-o-meter, events like Christmas or taking out a minor mortgage or loan.

The next thing they did was to place a number next to each event on an intensity scale, based on the data they had compiled. The numbers ranged from 100 at the highest to 11 at the lowest. For years, this "Social Readjustment Scale" has been used to predict the likelihood of becoming ill after an assault by stressful events. If the total score for events over the past year exceeded 300, you were more likely to become ill. If the score was less than 150, your risk was low.

Highest on the Holmes and Rahe list, with an intensity level of 100, was death of a spouse. Coming in second on the list was divorce at 73, followed by marital separation at 65. Imprisonment follows at 63, and being diagnosed with a major illness has an intensity level of 53.

So there it is. Divorce is the second most stressful experience we will ever face in our lives. It is a bona fide blockbuster. Indeed, divorce researcher E. Mavis Hetherington (from whom we'll hear more later) found in her enormous study of divorcing individuals that in the first year after divorce, doctor's visits doubled for men and tripled for women.

One family lawyer has famously observed, "Criminal lawyers see the worst people at their best; divorce lawyers see the best people at their worst." Little surprise here. When we are being squeezed by the vice of stress, whatever maladaptive behaviors that are in our nature will bloom. People react to stress in many, personally idiosyncratic, ways. Some become angry when feeling pressed, and their heat can scorch all around. Others withdraw entirely, finding the world to be overwhelming. There are the workaholics; the drinkers; the spenders; the eaters; and those whose brains become diffuse, and suddenly simple tasks become impossible. Some, like me, become withdrawn, and the world darkens for a time. Whatever your natural response to stress— and we all have them—none support you in being at your best.

Events that cause us stress mobilize our self-protective instincts. The greater the challenge, the more intense our focus on defense. Another extremely common form of self-defense when we feel under attack is *projection*. One simple way of describing this kind of defensive maneuver is that, when we are in conflict with another person, we maintain vigilant attention *on them*. Since we are in defensive mode, we are continually alert to the other's attack, or oncoming attack. It is impossible to feel comfortable when the messages you are receiving from another person are experienced as destructive to your very being. On top of that, you are going to be mightily pissed about having to worry about such attacks. With stressful interactions, then, comes singular attention on the other person. With this outer attention, there is little, if any, consideration of ourselves and whatever contribution we might have had in the conflict. This can be a self-perpetuating engine that drives both divorcing people nuts unless they are able to get an uninvolved third person to help them lower the heat. How that's done comes in later chapters. For now, it's just important to appreciate how dreadfully hard divorce is on people's psyches. In order to fully grasp the depth of the injury caused by divorce, we will need to understand "attachment" and its deep hold on us. This story begins decades ago and an ocean away.

WHAT *IS* ATTACHMENT?

John Bowlby was a proper English gentleman who came of age in the middle of the last century. Bowlby was a psychoanalytically trained psychiatrist. There were no social workers, marriage and family therapists, or even PhD clinical psychologists in those days. This was still the era in which Freudian analysis monopolized the world of mental health treatment. Bowlby lived in London during the heyday of psychoanalytic thought in that city. Sigmund Freud's daughter Anna and the formidable Melanie Klein practiced and taught there at the time. They were giants, and people were expected to worship at their thrones.

Yet, as Bowlby continued to work with young people, he was increasingly bothered by the emphasis in psychoanalytic circles on the child's *fantasy* life. Leaders in the field, like Freud and Klein, were absolutely committed to the idea that the distress we experience in our lives comes from the destructive fantasies that haunt us. They did not care at all what the actual experiences of infants and young children were. These were considered irrelevant. Bowlby had constant battles with the establishment over this. At one point, Klein supervised him as he worked with a young boy. The child's mother would bring the boy to sessions and then sit and wait—displaying incredible signs of the most intense anxiety. Bowlby found this important, but Klein harshly discouraged him from exploring that avenue. The child and his fantasy life (as opposed to his *actual* life) were the only things worth exploring. When the mother eventually was hospitalized with her own anxiety disorder, Bowlby was shocked to hear Klein express regret, only, that the child's ride to therapy was no longer available.

Bowlby's experience showed over and over again that distressed children had experienced actual trauma in their young lives, and a leading cause of distress seemed to be separation from a primary caregiver for a prolonged period. He wrote a paper about a handful of young thieves who seemed to be without remorse or conscience. In almost all other respects, these young people were pleasant and socially appropriate. There was just something *missing*. Almost every one of these young people had suffered prolonged separation from their primary caregiver when they were quite young.

Over time, he developed a theory about the importance of close, attuned connection with a caregiver and the impact of its absence. He called it *Attachment*. Bowlby found that there were four basic components of attachment. One was *proximity seeking*, which was the need of the baby for physical touch and contact with her caregiver. The second piece was that the baby used the caregiver as a *safe haven*, meaning that whenever there was a threat, the baby turned to her caregiver. For example, assume a baby is playing on the grass and there are five men sitting around, all very safe and pleasant. The child's father is the farthest away at that point. If there is a sudden sharp "crack" or frightening noise, the child will not turn to the nearest adult for protection, but will immediately look to her father. He is the child's safe haven. Third, the attachment relationship provides a *secure base* for the baby. So long as the caregiver is there and can be trusted to remain, the child feels free to explore her environment. If the connection is not trustworthy—if the caregiver can't naturally be expected to provide care—then the child might become preoccupied with the tenuous security provided. There will likely be less exploration. Finally, there is *separation distress*. When the caregiver is absent, the baby will vocalize, demonstrating the separation anxiety we have come to see commonly in small ones.

This need for a secure attachment with primary caregivers has been found to be a basic survival need, as insistent as the drive for food. In fact, one thing that started the whole push in research on attachment was the fact that babies in orphanages after World War I, who were given all the sustenance and comfort they needed, failed to thrive. Many died and the caregivers were stumped as to what could possibly cause this repeated and wrenching outcome. They eventually realized that the understaffed orphanages permitted workers to rarely hold these children and, even then for only a short time. A term was coined to describe this wasting away of babies. It was called "hospitalism." Over time we have learned that survival of the species depends on attachment and that all mammals have this need in their brains. The mother and child create an "attachment system." The baby smiles and coos, stimulating the reciprocal caregiving from the mother. In fact, researchers have found a specific part of the brain where these attachment needs arise.

ATTACHMENT AS A "HARDWIRED" EMOTION

Jaak (pronounced "Yak") Panksepp had a problem in his lab. Young mice born in cages that they'd never left were getting agitated when a particular worker came in to clean out their cages. Nobody could figure out why this occurred until someone in the lab realized that he had cats at home. It was the dander from these cats, which were on his clothes, that was causing the mice to go mad with fear. How could that be, though? These mice had never seen a cat. They probably couldn't even spell c-a-t. So how was it that they were freaking because of cat dander? This became just one of many examples which Panksepp and his colleagues found in the lab, showing the brain has built-in emotional reactions that reveal themselves with the right stimulus.

In his years of study, Panksepp found seven different emotional systems in the brain, each having a function necessary for survival and propagation of every mammalian species (including *us*). The *seeking* system drives the organism to explore his environment, seeking out resources necessary for survival. In humans it is experienced as curiosity, excitement, and motivation. The *rage* system establishes boundaries and pushes the organism to strike out when resources, territory, partners, and other necessities for survival are being restricted externally. The *fear* system is the flight part of "fight or flight." As the organism senses danger which might be overwhelming and threatens survival, this system triggers the action of retreat. The *lust* system drives the organism toward procreation.

The *care* system is activated by pregnancy and birth of offspring. The mother's body is flooded with the hormone *oxytocin*, which promotes care and nurturance. (Interestingly, a securely attached adult intimate relationship also floods us with *oxytocin*.) The *play* system promotes social bonding. Finally, the emotional system, which Panksepp called the *panic* system, but which I think is better described as the *attachment* system, is activated upon separation from important others.

In his work, Panksepp noticed that small baby mammals in his lab would emit a cry of distress when separated from their mothers. The cry would bring the mother back to the baby. He was able to evoke these cries of distress by stimulating a specific area of the brain with electrodes. (He also found six other neuron circuits in the brain that were the homes of the other basic emotions.) His work demonstrated that the need for attachment (like the other six emotional systems) is embedded in our brains.

Over the decades, into the '60s and '70s, we began to understand that this drive for attachment, which lies within a specific network of neurons, doesn't go away when we hit adolescence and beyond. The need for connection with another remains with us throughout our entire lives. When we have that securely attached relationship with that important *other*, we experience, as adults, all the steadiness of having a secure base, a safe haven, and calming touch. We have all experienced or witnessed the intense distress demonstrated when cut off from the person with whom we have formed our attachment bond. While we can surely gain a semblance of this security in various corners of our lives, there is only one place we feel all the benefits of attachment. That is in our primary intimate relationship. Our marriage (or non-marital partnership) is our *adult attachment relationship*.

It is with our intimate partner that we feel the calming influence of physical closeness and intimate touch. If our primary relationship is solid, we feel more emboldened to explore the world and show ourselves. Think of where you were when you first heard that the planes had hit the Twin Towers on 9/11. Did you call your husband/wife or primary partner? If so, that is an excellent example of the safe haven created by a securely attached primary relationship.

When the security of that relationship is threatened, we become distressed. The incredible promise of Emotionally Focused Therapy can help many couples lower that level of distress. However, many people can't manage to do it—and the bond ruptures. We separate. Our primary adult attachment relationship blows up, resulting in our suffering an "attachment injury." Attachment injuries are considered so deep, searing, and severe that at the time we can feel completely overwhelmed.

Writer Abigail Trafford called the six-month period after separation *Crazy Time*, and for good reason.

DIVORCE AS A PROCESS OVER TIME

Some time ago, *The Huffington Post* asked people to use one word to describe "divorce." Reponses ranged far and wide, but whether good or, for the most part, bad—or worse—it is an intense experience: *Pivotal. Painful. Torture. Supercallifragalistic-freakinsuckadocious. Heartbreaking (even though I initiated it). Rebirth. Freedom. Ex-marry. Destructive. Draining. Eye-opening. Sweet. Death. Overcomplicated. Hell. Option. Fate. Bittersweet. Blessing. Sobering. Brutal. Tragedy. Unending. Bye. Vengeful. Solution. Necessary. Expensive. Hard. Calm. Heartache. Amazing. Amputation. Numbing. Trying.*

One of the first things you might notice in the list, above, is that divorce is not considered a negative experience by everyone. Along with "Hell" and "Amputation" are "Rebirth" and "Calm." For those who find release from a bad marriage to be a "Blessing" or "Amazing," the attachment injury comes with the slow, corrosive destruction of the bond while it still feels alive to the other. For most, however, the transition to separation and divorce is a blow.

Divorce will shake your life up. There is no doubt about that. While painful and transformative, divorce does not have to be a life-destroying blow. For the overwhelming number of people it will not be. Experts who have studied divorce over the past thirty years come to the same conclusion: *Divorce is not an event. It is a process over*

_____

time. What begins as an emotionally overwhelming experience can ease until, wonder of wonders, you feel normal again. You are no longer preoccupied with making sense of your marriage and its demise. You don't feel angry so much of the time. Friends and family say you look happier and more relaxed. You are now able have a deep and rewarding (non-rebound) relationship.

That healing process doesn't occur in a week or a month. Most experts agree that the "divorce recovery process" takes about two years. This estimate is remarkably uniform among those who study divorce. That doesn't mean that a divorcing person is going to feel horrible for two years. The real hard part lasts around six months to a year, as mentioned earlier. After that, you have a steady climb to emotional freedom.

As Abigail Trafford says in *Crazy Time:*[9]

> *The loss through divorce is massive. It is the death of a relationship, a war with your past and the confrontation with your dreams of how you wanted your life to turn out. You learn things about your childhood, about your family and your friends. These are the dark secrets of divorce. Sometimes it's too much and most people go a little crazy for a while.*

That craziness, though, abates—*if given a chance*. As Trafford reminds us (if we need reminding), there are a ton of psychic resources diverted to the divorce adjustment process. If permitted to proceed over the ensuing months, without detours and crises, people usually turn out just fine. That's a tremendously comforting message for anyone in the throes of the craziness. One abiding reality that accompanies the fear, anxiety, and depression is that when you're in the middle of it, you honestly believe, at the bottom of your heart, that it will go on for the rest of your days. To hear that experts acknowledge how horrible it feels, but then assure that there is almost always a better day ahead, is balm for the wounded heart.

However, there's a "but" in all of this. You'll be okay in two years, *but* if you gouge more psychic wounds in one another's brains during the divorce process, all that energy that was going to be devoted to healing will now go to licking the most recently inflicted wounds. That's why you have to be mindful about how you manage your divorce process.

MAVIS HETHERINGSTON'S STUDY
OF THOUSANDS OF DIVORCING PEOPLE

Probably the biggest study of divorcing people was started in 1972 in Virginia by E. Mavis Hetherington.[10] Originally, she compared 72 preschool kids and their families, who were going through divorce, to non-divorcing families. By 1992, her study had grown to encompass 450 families and 900 children. She had the people keep diaries and fill out questionnaires, and she interviewed them periodically. Hetherington amassed a huge amount of data.

One thing she found was that after 24 months, people had settled into their stable, long-term pattern. Of all the divorcing people she studied, she described 40% as being "Good Enoughs." These were people who experienced divorce as a "speed bump" in their lives, but were able to regain stability and enter new relations with no real difficulty. Another 20% of her study group she described as "Enhancers." These were primarily women who tended to become more competent, self-fulfilled, and successful in their next marriages. Another 10% she categorized as "Competent Loners," people who didn't seek another relationship and seemed fine alone. Another group, quite large at the one-year point but later shrinking to an almost indistinguishable percentage, was made up of "Seekers." These people wanted to get into another relationship as quickly as possible and averaged around 40% of the total after one year. Seekers have great difficulty with basic domestic tasks and after the one-year mark are predominantly men. Hetherington found these men repeating their patterns established in the original marriage and moving in and out of successive relationships. "Libertines," also a small percentage, were symbolized by the classic guy who divorces, buys a sports car, and dates younger women. Again, after a period of such behavior, this group for the most part settles into the same conservative, married behavior that described their earlier relationship. Finally, about 10% of the Hetherington group were "Defeated." While a bit higher during the first turbulent months after the divorce, at the conclusion of 24 months the group had settled into the 10% ratio. These people were depressed and lost, never getting their lives on track. A number of obvious characteristics permeated the Defeated group, with poverty, mental or physical illness, and complete lack of social support predominating.

A full 90% of divorcing people in Hetherington's study made it through this harrowing life transition with their heads screwed on and their life energy intact. However, over and over, Hetherington and other divorce researchers identify one critical factor that can alter this otherwise smooth course. It won't be hard to guess what that might be:

> *Outstanding legal issues such as money, parenting, and visitation rights are major complicating factors in many divorces. And, of course, wherever there's a legal issue, there's a lawyer. Lawyers often protect and defend and advise. But their training in the adversarial process can stir up latent anger and resentment, turning a "friendly" or even a relatively neutral divorce into an ugly destructive one.*

Constance Ahrons, one of the country's experts on the psychological divorce process, has counseled:

> *A note needs to be made here about the impact of the legal system on the separation process. The separating spouses may interact with the legal system any time from pre-separation through late separation. But when they do, it can alter the separation process considerably. Much will depend, however, on which attorney and which method of dispute resolution the separating spouses choose. Although nearly all states now have no-fault legislation, the process of reaching an agreement on financial and custody issues is still usually resolved in an adversarial process. When the adversarial process interacts with the other processes of separating, it can increase the distress by adding an additional stressor to an already burdened system. It can cause the separating partners to cease communicating with each other and to continue their negotiations through their lawyers. In high conflict relationships this may be beneficial*

and even speed up the separation process. In other cases it can be detrimental, creating even more anger and conflict than was already present in the system.

The continuing theme is that if the conventional legal divorce doesn't mess up the relationship, people will be able to manage their divorce process, and come out the other side in relatively good shape.

FACING PSYCHOLOGICAL HURDLES

Divorce is particularly challenging for those struggling with a particular kind of emotional rigidity called a personality disorder. For years, the DSM (considered the "Bible" of mental health difficulties, describing virtually every problem from schizophrenia to nicotine addiction) had a separate category for personality disorders. As described by oft-cited article in the literature on divorce,

> *A personality disorder is a clinical term used to describe people who are "locked in" for many years with certain exaggerated personality traits that interfere with all aspects of their functioning in life.[11]*

Bill Eddy is a lawyer and social worker who has written and spoken extensively about "high conflict personalities." By this, he is referring to certain personality disorders that make the divorce process much more painful—for the sufferer, as well as others. Eddy says,

> *Perhaps half of all legal cases which go to trial today involve one or more parties with a high conflict personality— driven more by internal distress than external events…. The disputes of High Conflict Personalities are generally misunderstood and mishandled, and continue to escalate at a huge cost to our judicial system and our society—in terms of time, money, and emotional distress for all involved.[12]*

Eddy identifies four particular personality disorders as especially troublesome in the high pressure environment of divorce. These are the *Narcissistic* (characterized by a certainty that one is special and should be recognized as such—always the smartest, most talented person in the room), *Histrionic* (characterized by a drive to be the center of attention), *Antisocial* (characterized by a disregard of the rules which most of us operate by in society) and *Borderline* (characterized by an intense drive to merge psychologically with others, followed by intense anger upon failure of this effort). A fuller description of each can be found in this endnote.[13] Two of these (Narcissistic and Antisocial) reflect an absence of empathy that is particularly striking. It is as if that part of their brains which allow one to understand and appreciate the experience of another never really developed. Each will have its particular difficult style in the divorce arena.

The narcissistic personality will react with unreasonable demands, as their belief in their own entitlement presses to the forefront. The borderline personality, when faced with divorce, might tend to act with extremes of rage and grief, as the continued, pressing fear of betrayal is crystallized by their spouse's withdrawal. The antisocial personality will have little qualm about withholding information and acting in whatever way they can to exploit their spouse and "win" in an unwinnable situation. The histrionic personality will believe that their particular issues and concerns are different and special, and they will need constant reassurance.

Unfortunately, the combination of divorce (which is not a pothole but a *sinkhole* in the road) and the unreliable inner support which those struggling with personality disorders can rely upon, puts these people at greater risk. They will be overwhelmed by an urgent need to protect themselves. If the depressed person gets depressed under stress, the anxious person is flooded with anxiety, the angry person rages, then the personality disordered person *gets stuck*.

Substance abuse creates another insurmountable hurdle for those trying to make good decisions at the end of their relationship. There is *no way* a parent will feel comfortable leaving the children in the care of an active alcoholic or drug user—for good reason, too, as the addicted person craves the drink or the hit so insistently that everything else fades into the background. An active alcoholic will get behind the wheel of an automobile, secure in the belief that their driving is not impaired. This is, you will certainly agree, a problem. Yet the nature of divorce disputes might blind the addicted person to this fact. In divorce each person struggles with responsibility and the burden of blame over the end of the marriage. Substance abuse is a clear, identifiable behavior and feels like an objective proof of blame. Put yourself in that person's shoes—would *you* embrace the blame that accompanies the labeling and dive right into that pool of shame? Thus, in an adversarial divorce context, substance abuse might be strongly denied. How will the non-addicted parent react to denial on the part of the substance abuser? Likely the intensity of the anxiety and accusation will increase. This is why substance abuse is a particularly vexing problem in adversarial divorce and why mediation and collaborative law may be ideal forums for working out these issues, as we will see later.

It is important to appreciate that domestic abuse is completely antithetical to a divorce process that is mutually respectful. An adequate settlement, without the assistance of strong counsel, is impossible. The ability of the domestic abuser to empathize with his partner is nonexistent.

Divorce is hard enough for the emotionally unafflicted and stout of heart. For those who enter this field of emotional tripwires weighted down by the rigidity of a personality disorder, or instability imposed by substance abuse, or the dominance and submission of domestic violence, it is certain they will stumble and fall. These issues must be addressed if there is any chance at achieving a decent agreement without the pain of a courtroom drama.

A good way to think about all this is that legal divorce is a process of creating boundaries of behavior. Those who are challenged as described here have great difficulty recognizing and conforming to boundaries. That, ultimately, is the job of lawyers and courts. Their process is to impose clear boundaries of conduct and to enforce them with punishment if they are violated. That, at base, is their value.

EMOTIONAL RESOLUTION

During the divorce transition, a dense cloud of fog (or is it smog?) descends over our day-to-day existence. The stress is so intense that we can barely manage to put one foot in front of the other. The emotions that buffet our lives are wicked. If the separation is accompanied by the betrayal of infidelity, it can feel like we have been shoved out of a window at forty stories. The foundation of our lives has been ripped away—we feel vertigo and nausea and we *know* we are going to die.

Yet, we don't die. Divorce is not the end of the world. While the trauma of severing an intimate bond is quite profound, time does allow us to heal the deep wound. If you ask someone who has suffered through diagnosis, treatment, and recovery from cancer, they will likely tell you they learned a lot about themselves and their inner resources. They are better and stronger for the experience. Still, all things considered, most would prefer to have passed on the opportunity, if given a chance. Divorce is like that for most.

Yet, as painful and destabilizing as divorce might be, avenues exist for achieving an outcome that feels healthy and supportive of both oneself, the children…and even the other person. The next chapters will introduce us to what has been learned over the past two decades about how to do divorce right.

TAKEAWAYS

- **The Psychological Divorce Process will usually extend beyond the conclusion of the Legal Divorce Process. Expect it. Prepare for it. Manage it.**
- **Fewer times in life call out more insistently for psychological counsel. If you do not have a therapist, find one who has some experience counseling people through divorce. Divorce will almost always stir up long-protected or compartmentalized fears, self-negating thoughts, shames, or other hidden (even to ourselves) psychological challenges. You're human. It comes with the territory. This is an excellent time to finally address those things inside which have held you back from personal well-being.**
- **During the stress of the divorce transition, we often limit our thoughts of the future to worry. There is more there for us. Start a list of the things you want in the future. Don't limit yourself to concerns about an item being realistic. Just write it down. Take these to a counselor or trusted friend and get their help in determining what is realistic. Set goals for what will make you happy, and gather the**

resources to help you embark on that journey. This is essential for recovery from divorce.

CHAPTER 5

If You Can't Avoid Divorce, Do It Right

<u>Beth</u>

Looking back, Beth doesn't know how she survived the year after she left Adam. She was unbelievably guilty during that time. Seeing the emails between him and Susie helped a little—she was able to be angry sometimes instead of guilty. Still, good feelings of any kind were far beyond her grasp. She was glad that Adam chose to move out and didn't fight her over who stayed and who left. Telling Lilly and Jason was a wrenching experience. Beth was on her own in that one. Adam had said, "You're the one who's throwing me out, *you* tell them." He'd say to the children, "It was Mom's decision. Ask her about it." Beth couldn't really explain to herself why she had ended it, much less explain to Lilly and Jason, so she did the lame, "Daddy and I just don't love each other the way married people are supposed to," and then she took the blowback. (Well, it *felt* lame, although it's what she had read in the books and what Delores had suggested, as well.) Lilly was really angry at her for about three months, but when Lilly saw that her father already had a girlfriend, her heart softened toward her mother. He had introduced Susie as his "friend," but Lilly wasn't an idiot. She knew what was going on. Beth and Lilly had sat on her daughter's bed, and she had held her daughter close while she sobbed.

Even though Beth didn't have any romantic feelings for Adam any longer, she felt shaken to the core at the thought of his sharing his bed with someone so soon. Everything was up in the air and it kept her up at night—that is, unless she downed three glasses of wine. Then she was able to fall into fitful, light sleep. Adam had continued to deposit his check into the joint account and they managed. She had to stretch the food budget out and cursed herself for deciding to get divorced with an adolescent boy in the house—he of the bottomless pit for a stomach. Friday nights curled up on the couch watching a movie with the kids was the best time. Sitting alone in the tomb-like silence of her house when the kids were with Adam was the worst. If it hadn't been for Daisy, Beth is sure she would have gone crazy. Daisy had another friend, ridiculously named Summer, who was also going through divorce and suggested they go out for dinner one night. Summer got drunk and spent half the time bashing her husband, and Beth begged off further engagements with her.

Sometimes, what kept her up at night—when even the better part of a bottle of Pinot Gris couldn't help—was money. There wasn't going to be enough. She would have to get a job. Adam's lawyer was pressing for her to go to work immediately, but the only thing she could think of doing was receptionist work for a doctor's office. The idea of being a forty-year-old barista at Starbucks horrified her…although there *were* benefits. Nothing would pay her enough in the long run, and they certainly weren't "career paths." Would she be able to keep the house? If not, where would she and the kids go? If so, how was she going to pay for the new roof that they had held off on for three years? The water stains in the ceiling in the family room gave her nightmares—when she was able to fall asleep. She knew that the idea of buying one shred of new clothing in the next couple of years was a fantasy. Would she have to sell off her jewelry to survive? How was she going to pay for her lawyer? She was glad she had a Volvo, which was reliable. Although, it *did* have 85,000 miles on it, and some major maintenance was due. If only she could send out a notice, "Getting Divorced," and put a hold on everything for six months until she got her head straight—but that wasn't going to happen.

THE GOOD AND THE BAD DIVORCE

Up to this point, if you are the *Dumper*, you have considered the hardships of divorce and the ways that this path could have been avoided. If you are the *Dumpee*, you are struggling with this new and painful reality. Whatever your route, you're here—with heavy heart to be sure, but there is no getting around it. So, what are your next steps?

The first thing to understand with crystalline clarity is knowing that divorce is not a failure of personal integrity. There are certainly voices within our society who will dispute that, but don't let yourself succumb to the life-sapping guilt and destructive self-denial that these messengers will transmit. The sign of integrity is not *whether* you divorce—it is *how you divorce*. There are right and wrong ways to begin this process. One book about traumatic divorce shares this perspective,[14]

> *Just as a marriage can be deemed as more or less successful or as having failed, so can a divorce be seen as being more or less successful or as having failed to accomplish its purpose. In a successful divorce, the adults are able to work through their anger, disappointment, and loss in a timely manner and terminate their spousal relationship with each other (legally and emotionally), while at the same time retaining or rebuilding their parental alliance with and commitment to their children...*
>
> *There are kind and humane ways to end a relationship. There are also particularly brutal and traumatic ways to part...sudden desertion, the humiliating discovery of a lover, uncharacteristic violence, secret plotting and planning. One man took his wife to dinner for their twentieth wedding anniversary and gave her his gift: a petition for divorce. A man returning from overseas military service at Christmas was greeted by a tape recorded message from his wife saying*

she's fallen in love with another man. A grieving woman returned from her father's funeral to find that her husband had stripped the house of all their possessions and left with the children. An older man walked out for a pack of cigarettes and never came back. A young woman missed the last bus home from work and decided then and there she could never return. While recovering from emergency surgery for breast cancer, a woman was informed by her husband that he wanted a divorce.

I have seen partners who are finished with the marriage but who don't want to be the "bad guy" who left: they create a nearly intolerable marital environment, forcing the other to leave, so they can say, "She left me!" Some are so overwhelmed by their anger and the pain of abandonment that a *ton* of emotional energy goes into thwarting the errant partner. Unrealistic demands, intentional violation of small agreements (or of large agreements in chronic, small ways, like bringing the children back late or delaying support payments for an extra couple of days), and unnecessary sniping in email exchanges that you *know* is going to upset the other, are just some of the ways a normally rough transition can be made worse.

As mentioned earlier, lawyers can naturally get pulled into the fray. You might think of it as a mysterious, energetic process that creeps up on the participants like a toxic fog. Husband and wife separate. They are both angry and cannot let go of the destructive cycle that eroded their marital bond. The heat of their interaction is at a chronic, sub-molten level. This fractured energy is then transmitted to their lawyers. Indeed, lawyers who otherwise get along and have great fondness and respect for one another start lobbing what a colleague calls "nastygrams" back and forth via email. When lawyers get involved with a couple divorcing, they enter that family system and, as with all family systems, the anxiety is easily generated back and forth, to and from all segments.

TAKING CARE OF YOURSELF
DURING YOUR DIVORCE

Before talking about a new kind of lawyer and legal divorce, let's look at nine basic rules, which are critical for people who want to navigate this transition in a self-sustaining and humane manner.

1.   *Get Personal Support*

Divorcing people *can't go through this alone.* There are a number of sources of support, and as many of these should be utilized as possible. Therapy is almost indispensable during this exquisitely wrenching period of your life. If there is a current relationship with a trusted mental health counselor, consider yourself lucky. If there is not, seriously consider finding someone who has some level of expertise dealing with people going through the divorcing process. You may think yourself crazy at times, and having a professional, who can sit with you and help you understand that your reactions are *normal*, is exceedingly helpful. Therapists can provide a safe place to explore your current experience, reality test in a nonjudgmental fashion, and help problem-solve. Not being emotionally involved in your current life crisis allows this person to have clarity and compassion. This is, of course, a best-case scenario. We must be careful that our therapist does not contribute to an uncompromising and rigid position of victimhood and deep umbrage. Experienced divorce counselors have observed:[15]

> *Mental health professionals who undertake individual counseling and psychotherapy for a separating spouse are usually privy to only one view of the family problem.... In support of a seemingly powerless, depressed, or abused spouse, they can encourage an uncompromising, aggressive stance that results in prolonged disputes over the post-divorce care of children.... They can also unwittingly endorse their client's distorted views of the divorce situation and consolidate their client's polarized negative image of the ex-spouse.*

Family and friends are another important source of support. As with any life crisis, there is a tendency to talk ceaselessly about what you are going through. It can burn people out over the long haul. That is why a therapist can be invaluable during this passage. Yet, to avoid family and friends because of embarrassment or fears of being a burden is usually a mistake. You need social support.

2.   *Exercise Self-Care*

When your world turns upside-down, you will likely be less inclined to do the things that can help keep you grounded. First, as noted above, don't isolate yourself. In addition to that, make sure you are eating well. Depression and anxiety can dampen appetite and you might not eat as much as you would otherwise. However, what you *do* eat needs to be healthy and sustaining. Avoid sugar overload. Take care in the amount of alcohol you use. Start your day with a healthy breakfast, rather than skipping it or limiting yourself to coffee and some sugary concoction. Find a time in your life to relax. Ask for help with your children so you can spend time engaging in some enjoyable, relaxing, and self-soothing activity at least two or three times per week. Get as much sleep as you are able. If you have difficulty falling asleep, be aware of the television you watch before lights go out. If you have an iPod or other MP3 device, listen to relaxing music or a meditation download. There are many CDs and podcasts that are supportive of relaxation. A current podcast I like very much is *Meditation Oasis*, but there are scores of websites and CDs in local bookstores that carry this kind of material. See your doctor if you need temporary pharmaceutical help sleeping.

By all means, find an avenue for exercise. If you are a member of a gym, go in at least three times each week. If you do yoga, do yoga. If exercise is not part of your routine and you feel out of shape, then start taking half-hour walks in your neighborhood. There is ample evidence that exercise helps alleviate depression, so take advantage of your physical body and do what you can. If you have a difficult time summoning up the motivation to do it yourself, get a buddy to do it with you. Keep in mind, not feeling like doing this is not a reason to avoid it. You probably *won't* feel like doing it, but you must do whatever you can to take care of yourself during this particularly stressful time in your life.

3. *Keep Your Children in Their Own Generation*

Sometimes your children will be the only people around you for much of the time. They afford wonderful companionship and distraction. Many parents, however, make the grave mistake of treating their children like contemporaries. These people tell themselves that their children are extraordinarily mature, so they will share personal concerns with them. When parents confide in their children, it places an unmanageable burden on their little shoulders. Never, ever, think your child is a friend, no matter how mature you believe him to be. Your kids don't need a friend as much as they need a parent, no matter their age. They can turn to their contemporaries for friendship and peer support. Hopefully they *are* doing that. Almost always, children desperately need to feel safe to love both parents. You need to allow them to do this.

Three crucial messages that children need to hear when their parents are separating are (1) it is not their fault, (2) they will lose neither parent in this process, and (3) this is an issue to be dealt with by the parents. The kids do not need to know how the two of you have come to this point. Now, if you are divorcing your husband because he has kicked you to the curb and is now involved with a woman fifteen years younger than you, keeping your pain and sense of cosmic injustice to yourself will be exceedingly difficult. Many parents in this situation ask, "How can I have any integrity and lie to my children? It's his fault our family is blowing up." Yet, choosing not to expose your children to this particularly adult pain might be the highest demonstration of personal integrity and your love for them. While you may feel they need to know the truth, they don't need to know about conduct that ended the marriage, particularly if it might cause them to reject the other parent. This will damage their young psyches. If they end up with their own issues with the other parent, they can take it up in the most appropriate way with that person. Maybe they should have a few sessions with a family therapist. Maybe you can coach them on how to talk with the other parent. You've got to let your kids be kids, though. That's their role in your family, whether you are intact or divorced.

4. *Avoid Overuse of Alcohol and Drugs*

Even though this was mentioned earlier, it bears a strong separate category. Alcohol is a great numbing agent. Up to a point, it might help relax you. If you can have a glass of wine, or two, for that purpose, why not go ahead? Many of us, however, find it difficult to limit our intake to those two glasses and find ourselves drinking to inebriation on a consistent basis. This will turn into a major problem since (1) alcohol is a depressant, and (2) it turns off the brakes in your brain and lets your emotions take the wheel. Neither of these effects will help you during this crisis period in your life. Pharmaceutical substances like benzodiazepines, which are a class that describes many common anti-anxiety drugs, are seriously addictive, and the "rebound effect," which will make your symptoms even stronger if you stop the drug, will hook you. If you have a serious problem (like divorce), involvement with addictive substances won't solve the problem. It will pile an even more serious problem onto the former. So be thoughtful around their use. Consult with a doctor or naturopath, who will discuss calming agents clearly with you.

5. *Be Careful of the Rebound Relationship*

Probably nothing can feel better than connecting with someone who finds you attractive, sexy, interesting, and fun after you have been in relationship doldrums for months or years. You will be amazed at the things you both have in common. All the hungers you experienced over years of deprival will be satisfied: "He loves to go out at night." "She's athletic and takes hikes with me." "I can't believe I can spend an entire day with someone and not fight." "He loves to sit quietly and just read." "She's not jealous if I banter with a waitress." And, of course, there's the sex. Since couples in distress and headed for divorce often haven't touched one another tenderly or sensually in years, nothing feels better than having good sex again. The attraction is usually overpowering, and you feel new and alive. While good feelings are a blessing and a balm during this difficult time, there are a couple of yellow flags flapping in the wind you should be alert to.

How does it feel for you to be alone? Is it so frightening that you will jump at a decent opportunity to join with someone else as soon as you can? While there is unquestionably much that you can learn about yourself in a relationship, many of our life lessons can only come if we are on our own for a while. Rushing into a relationship again shortchanges us, denying ourselves the opportunity to learn that we can manage and even flourish on our own. Without this confidence in ourselves, we will cling ever more tightly to later relationships that might turn sour or even destructive to our well-being.

6.   *Be Mindful — You Are Not Your Emotions*

Divorce is a time when emotions and repetitive, invasive thoughts seem to run rampant. We are raised in this society to believe that we *are* our feelings. When we are angry or scared or embarrassed, we are inseparable from those experiences, and we naturally identify closely with them. Over the last few years, however, a growing body of important writing has emerged that questions this assumption. The idea that binds all of this thinking together is *mindfulness*. Daniel Siegel, MD, a psychotherapist, neuroscientist, and promoter of mindfulness, has scoured the literature on the subject, and he describes what seem to be five factors that define mindfulness:[16]

(1) Being aware of one's inner experience of emotions, but not reacting to them. ("I am angry right now. Hmm, what's that about?")

(2) Remaining present with sensations and feelings even when they are unpleasant or painful. ("I have such grief over the end of my relationship. I won't divert my attention or numb the experience with a distraction or alcohol.")

(3) Acting with awareness/not on automatic pilot. Slowing down to act with intention. ("I am engaged and conscious of activities like eating, driving, listening to others.")

(4) Describing/labeling with words. ("I don't just feel 'frustrated' or 'bad' but understand that I am experiencing 'confusion' or 'fear' or even 'shame' right now.")

(5) Nonjudgmental experience. ("Whatever I am experience is all right. I don't need to feel guilty or inadequate for what is going on inside. What I am feeling isn't inappropriate or wrong.")

Siegel goes on to discuss how we might soothe ourselves through "discernment," as a key part of mindfulness:

> *Discernment is a form of dis-identification from the activity of your mind: As you become aware of sensations, images, feelings, and thoughts (SIFT) you come to see these activities of the mind as waves at the surface of the mental sea. From this deeper place within your mind, this internal space of mindful awareness, you can just notice the brain waves at the surface as they come and go. This capacity to disentangle oneself from the chatter of the mind, to discern that these are "just activities of the mind," is liberating and for many, revolutionary. At its essence, this discernment is how mindfulness may help alleviate suffering.*

There are many avenues you may take to develop this liberating appreciation for the transitory nature of thoughts and emotions. A number of excellent books are currently available. One may also pursue a therapeutic relationship with a counselor who emphasizes mindfulness in their practice. Mindfulness meditation CDs or classes are also helpful.

7. *Take Your Allies With a Grain of Salt*

While social support is vitally important whenever we are going through a challenging time in our lives, we must still be careful not to allow these loving and well-meaning people to cause deeper confusion through their efforts.

Experts in post-divorce adjustment have observed:[17]

> *The social world of the divorcing couple is often split in two at the time of the separation, as common friends either withdraw in discomfort or take sides with one partner or the other in an attempt to support and help. As the details of this once private and intimate relationship are shared with potentially supportive and sympathetic others, the norms of privacy and exclusivity that surround and protect the marital relationship break down and dissipate. Through long hours*

of conversation, the history of the marriage is reinterpreted and rationalizations for the separation are sought, formulated, and confirmed. This is essentially a process of making meaning from the unhappy sequence of precipitating events, coming to terms with what went wrong, and trying to establish who is to blame for the failure of the marriage.

Unfortunately, significant others, family, and friends usually hear only one version of the breakup. With information garnered from only one spouse, these others can be drawn into parental disputes, become outraged, and seek to right a wrong and protect the parent from being further "victimized" by the divorcing spouse.

Many is the time I and colleagues have been confronted by a frightened divorce client who regales us with stories of incredible outcomes achieved by friends, or legal opinions rendered by someone whose only claim to expertise is their own sad, desperate divorce experience. Be careful about the information you let in, as those who advocate taking a strong position and going for "what you are entitled to" might fuel an avoidable war that will leave everyone in your family wounded and bitter.

8. *Take the Long View*
One characteristic of depression or severe stress is that our vision narrows down to the moment. We believe, deeply, that the pain or confusion we are experiencing will be perpetual. It's the state of our lives, we believe. This frame of reference can cause deeper depression and desperation. Yet, these beliefs are untrue. As Hetherington has said, after years of studying this process and its participants, the most important lesson she divined from her work is "The Resilience Lesson:"[18]

Divorce and remarriage initially are experienced as stressful transitions by both children and adults. Looking back, many parents and adult offspring describe divorce as the most painful event in their lives, but they also say that they were able to adapt to their new situation and are currently leading reasonably gratifying lives. About 75 to 80 percent of adults and children show few serious long-term problems in adjustment following divorce and are functioning within normal range. Many who have long-term problems after divorce had problems that preceded the break-up.

For almost all people experiencing the trauma of divorce, there will come a day, two years down the line (maybe more, maybe less) when they will look back and *know* that they have come through it. Their feet will be firmly planted on the ground. They will be in a relationship again. There will be a comfortable and confident knowledge that their connection with their children is strong and stable. They feel good about themselves.

While proceeding through the challenges of the divorce transition, it is hard to keep your eyes on that future; you are so preoccupied with the overwhelming challenges of the *now*. That is why it is helpful to create a mantra for yourself that "It's all going to turn out fine." Put it on Post-its and stick it on your bathroom mirror. Repeat this to yourself repeatedly on a daily basis. Surround yourself with people who can reflect that back to you. You'll get through this, if you take care of yourself.

9.   *Do the Legal Divorce Right*

One of the greatest misconceptions rampant among those considering divorce is that they must avoid lawyers. The common view is that lawyers will only exacerbate the conflict and drive up the costs of divorce. You either get a lawyer or you don't. However, this is a misleading view. It's not like an "on" or "off" switch. There are a number of pathways through the thickets of legal divorce, using greater or lesser constellations of professional support. Depending on your needs and internal resources, you will find an avenue that works best for you. The old-fashioned method of *both people hire lawyers who work it out (or duke it out)* is not the only way. The following schematic summarizes the choices, from the least expensive option, with a minimum amount of professional involvement, to the most expensive, with the entire legal cavalry mounted up and charging into battle.

THE CONTINUUM OF DIVORCE DISPUTE RESOLUTION

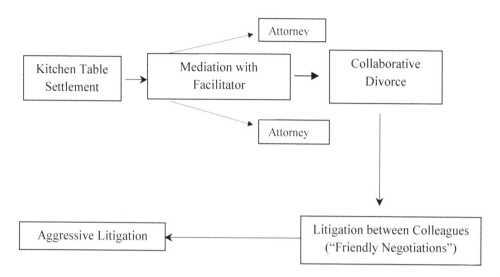

Some people are able to sit down together without any professional help and work through the details of their legal divorce. Since divorce is far and away the most common legal process in our courts, many people who need to dissolve their marriages don't have the money to hire lawyers, so they choose to do it themselves. It's a tricky decision, because on one hand it is important to hold onto scarce resources, yet, on the other hand, this *is* a *legal process*, and to go through it without any guidance from someone who understands the law and how documents need to be drafted and processed can be a mistake. Still, this is an effective option for people who have not been married long and who have no children (or no issues regarding parenting if there are kids) and little by way of assets or liabilities.

The next level of professional involvement is mediation, which will be discussed in more detail later. Essentially, for people who are able to manage their emotions and where power in the relationship is fairly well balanced, the assistance and guidance of a mediator can be a perfect solution. This approach allows people to talk about their needs and concerns and arrive at solutions in a safe environment. They should also work with lawyers who provide "unbundled legal services," which is a way to selectively employ the services of a lawyer without slapping down a retainer fee of a few thousand dollars and having to accept the "full meal deal."

However, many couples find it nearly impossible to sit together and discuss the terms of their divorce. Emotions might be too high. One or both people might feel overmatched by the other in terms of personality or knowledge of finances. When people need support that is more active and consistent throughout the process, Collaborative Divorce is an excellent option. Given the fact that it has been around for twenty-five years, has an extremely robust international community and organization (The International Academy of Collaborative Professionals), and maintains a strong presence in nearly every state, it is a wonder that people are still unaware of its existence and benefits. This approach will also be explained in greater detail in a later chapter, but suffice it to say here, mediation and collaborative divorce are much smarter ways to proceed through this life transition than the conventional approach (otherwise, I wouldn't have written this book!).

Which, of course, leads us to the conventional approach. This can be broken down into two categories. In each, the divorcing individuals essentially turn their divorce over to the professionals to work out. The lawyers talk to each other and manage the process. Outcomes are gauged almost entirely from the vantage of what a judge would do. Options that would work for a particular couple, but which a court would never order, are dismissed or discouraged. In the first, the process is collegial between lawyers, and unwarranted hostility and aggravation is avoided. Still, as was explained in painful detail earlier, the very structure of this process leads people to alienation and intense self-protection. The second option will be for each person to hire an aggressive "pit bull," "bulldog," "barracuda," or some other aggressive animal. When placed at the mercy of these lions and tigers and bears (oh my!), one can be sure that the cost of immersion in this battle, both financially and psychologically, will be high.

Probably the chief argument for resorting to less adversarial approaches is the damage that conventional approaches visit upon children. Since this is such a critical concern, let's take a moment to talk about children and how they process this seismic life transition.

CHAPTER 6

Why Do It Right?
Divorce and Children

<u>Lilly and Jason</u>

Really, Lilly could not believe how *selfish* her parents were. For years they'd been on her to work hard, stay out of trouble, get good grades—the whole "good girl" menu. She had done it, but it wasn't easy. Especially now. Jayden broke up with her last month, and he was already dating that slut, Deanne. It was literally the worst time of her life. On top of that, it was her last year before high school and the classes were getting harder, especially the math. She could hardly keep up, and texting about Jayden and all the other stuff with her best friend, Alex, was a necessary part of her night if she was going to keep her sanity. Her brother, Jason, was completely oblivious, spending all of his time in his room on his computer with his nerdy loser friends playing those stupid games.

When her mother had sat down with her and Jason and told them about the divorce, Lilly had thought, "Well, duh. It's not like it wasn't totally obvious for months." She had to know why, though. Why did her parents decide to mess up her world? This not loving each other like married people, blah blah blah, wasn't helping.

Why? She never got a good answer to that question, so the whole thing seemed stupid...and selfish. Having her daddy move out felt so weird. Having him come to the house in the morning to drive her and Jason to school was even weirder. Daddy was always so easygoing and nice. She could not understand why her mother wanted to divorce him. When she'd ask him, he'd just say, "Ask your mother," and then he'd change the subject. He would take them out to dinner, rather than cook something at his apartment—her father in an apartment was yet another weird thing. One night, they were joined by her daddy's girlfriend, Susie. They didn't <u>act</u> like boyfriend and girlfriend, but it was so completely obvious—mostly because they seemed so uncomfortable. Who's uncomfortable sitting with a "friend"? Susie wasn't around when they stayed at her daddy's place, which was a huge relief. Another weird thing—Daddy would sleep on the couch and Jason would sleep in his bed, and Lilly had her own room. One thing she *definitely* did not like was that there was no more Daddy/Lilly time. She only saw him on weekends and on Wednesday nights for dinner, and it was always with that loser, Jason, along. Before the divorce, she and her father had taken a one-week driving trip together every summer. He told her that this wouldn't be happening anymore. Her parents had also promised her that she'd get a Facebook account when she turned fourteen, but now her mother said they weren't going to be able to do that until she turned fifteen and the divorce was all settled. Lilly really hated that. She hated a lot about this divorce. The biggest pain she had was that it *made no sense*. Her parents didn't fight, and there didn't seem to be any reason to cause this disaster.

Lilly would harbor a lot of this resentment into her twenties, when she would see a counselor for the first time and begin to unpack a lot of these feelings.

Jason found his sister basically annoying. He thought she was a drama queen. People get divorced. His best friend Ben's parents got divorced two years ago. That had been a battle that made *World of*

Warcraft seem tame. Ben and his brother had been visited by some woman who talked with them about the divorce, and then a judge had said they had to go back and forth between their mom's house and their dad's house. Ben didn't like his dad, and he thought the bouncing around, when he had a perfectly good room in his own house, was just dumb. Jason was lucky because he liked his dad, and there hadn't been a big fight about where he and "the princess" would live. He thought his dad's girlfriend, Susie, was nice, though he figured that was why his mom was so sad most of the time. While it made him feel guilty, he kind of liked being with his dad more than his mom, because his dad was basically chill, and that fit Jason's personality. Also, his mom started laying a lot more chores on him at the house. Lilly didn't have to do anything, and it was all on him. Mom would yell at him if he left his dishes in the sink or if his room had a speck of dust anywhere. There was just more tension at his mom's house than his dad's. Maybe when he was fifteen, he'd get to choose where he could live, but that was still four years off, so he'd just keep his head down and see what happened.

KIDS' DIVORCE ISN'T ADULTS' DIVORCE

One force that has pushed lawyers for divorcing couples to seek an approach that will ease their level of conflict was the dawning realization that clients' best interests were much wider than just more money in the bank or hours with a child. Unlike many other forms of litigation, divorce is marked by the reality that if you've got kids, you're going to be seeing an awful lot of your ex-partner for a long, long time. If a divorce is conducted in the more conventional fashion, former partners will often gouge great psychic wounds in each other and then have to deal with this person they resent with venom and spite. How does this impact kids? Almost certainly—almost always—not well.

Except for a small percentage of cases, so as to be almost infinitesimal, children love both of their parents. For sure, there may be an affinity toward one or the other, but very, very few kids fail to love each parent deeply. What happens to a child who gets the message that to love mom is a betrayal of dad, or to love dad is a betrayal of mom, or *both*? To be sure, almost all but the most emotionally disturbed adult will state clearly that they make a point to avoid fighting in front of the children. They never say overtly negative things about the other parent to, or in front of, the children. While, of course, it's good that parents aren't traumatizing their kids with raging fights in front of them or using nasty put-downs of the other parent, this is only a small part of how children get a message from the adults in their lives.

Children have exquisitely sensitive emotional antennae when it comes to their parental figures. After all, if a parent is displeased with them, that's usually not going to bode too well for the child. Kids pick up on their parents' moods and attitudes as they may shift on a second-by-second basis. When a child returns to his mother's home from being with Dad and says excitedly, "Mommy, Daddy took me to the baseball game today," does Mom say quietly, "Go wash your hands for dinner," and then mention nothing more about it? If the mention of Dad causes Mom pain, she can't hide it. The deeper the pain, the clearer the signal.

One expert on children and divorce observes,[19]

> *The research literature concerning children who have experienced their parents' divorce is clear. Once basic financial needs are met, the greatest social risk to children is prolonged conflict between their parents.*

She goes on to quote the suggestion from divorce expert Joan Kelly (from whom we'll hear more, soon):

> *The intensity and frequency of parent conflict, the style of conflict, its manner of resolution and the presence of buffers to ameliorate the effects of high conflict are the most important predictors of child adjustment.*

Or as noted by another expert,[20]

> *When children are free to love both their parents without conflict of loyalty, to have access to them both without fear of losing either, they can get on with the totally absorbing business of growing up, on schedule. They can learn to master the tasks that life places before them with confidence and a sense of security.*

A loyalty conflict of any depth will seriously mess with their little brains. Daniel Siegel tells us that this is *literally* true. Research over the last twenty-five years has revealed the presence of *mirror neurons* in our brains, which do a number of different jobs. Siegel addresses one of these functions when he says that these brain cells should be called *sponge neurons*, "because you soak up like a sponge the intention of another person." He goes on to say,[21]

> *...there are neural circuits that help us map out the mind and intention of another person and ultimately enable us to resonate with the other, so that two people become a "we." This resonance is essential for healthy attachment. This is how the baby "feels felt" by the caregiver. These resonance circuits also enable us to perceive the intentional state of another and link not only our internal states, but our behaviors as well. The important thing is this: if a parent has the intention to harm another parent, even if they do not actually do anything, kids are going to pick that up. They will literally soak that intention in. To have one parent have a negative intention towards another is toxic. It is that simple. It is toxic.*

When children's sense of safety and security is threatened, there is a much higher risk that they will succumb to an array of challenges like drug or alcohol abuse, premature sexuality, depression, petty crime, academic struggles, and other worrisome behaviors. So ask yourself, is it in your best interests to fight for what you are "legally entitled to," if, in doing so, it is such a challenge to your former spouse's well-being that *deep and avoidable* resentments brew and *these* create an environment that will result in any number of painful development challenges for your child? Do you want to expend a ton of emotional energy dealing with the fallout of your divorce for years to come, rather than getting on with it? That is the "paradigm shift" for divorcing people. When either the lawyer or the client, or both, have a hard time making that shift, trouble's on the horizon.

JUDITH WALLERSTEIN
AND
HER WORK ON KIDS AND DIVORCE

Judith Wallerstein was a much-loved and respected expert in the field of divorce and its impact on children. She died in 2012 at the ripe old age of 93.

She and Joan Kelly began a long-term study of 60 families and their 131 children in 1971. The result was an eloquent and insightful book, *Surviving the Breakup: How Children and Parents Cope with Divorce*. Wallerstein later wrote a 25-year follow-up, with Julia Lewis and Sandra Blakeslee, *The Unexpected Legacy of Divorce*. While Wallerstein's views on the impact of divorce on children tend to be more pessimistic than Hetherington's, there is so much that is valuable in her work that divorcing parents would be remiss in not becoming familiar with her observations and insights.

One point made repeatedly by Wallerstein is that the child's experience of divorce is far different from his parents'. While at least one of the parents views the transition from an intact family to be a remedy for deep unhappiness and a step toward a hopeful future, this view is shared by a tiny number of children. For kids, almost always, the divorce of their parents is a catastrophe—one that can be weathered, but a catastrophe in the moment nonetheless. In fact, Wallerstein notes that children, even through adolescence and young adulthood, *still* maintain fantasies of their parents' reconciliation.

One cannot read Wallerstein and Kelly's *Surviving the Breakup* and be unmoved by their poignant descriptions of children coping with divorce. The three- to five-year-olds they observed were bewildered, frightened, and fell back on fantasy and denial as coping devices. For an example of their evocative observations, here is a representative passage, describing one little girl:

> *Linda, age four, appeared in our office, an attractive, blond, well-groomed child. When asked about what was happening at home, she solemnly explained that her father was living in the city because he didn't like Mommy, and that Mommy felt bad because she (Mommy) still liked Daddy. As was characteristic of many of the children, Linda*

accomplished her sober and dutiful recitation of the events of the household with play which belied her spoken words.

Linda played in an eerie silence. All the usual and familiar sounds with which children accompany their play was absent. She constructed a serene scene in which mother and father lay in bed together. The children played happily in an adjoining room as the baby slept peacefully in the crib. As the narrative developed, the mother arose to make a bountiful breakfast and the little boy generously brought a bowl of cereal to another child.

At the second meeting the child again arranged a happy family scene. The family members all watched television together. The father held the baby on his lap and the baby was comfortable in the father's arms. The children were seated on the floor in front of their parents. After the show the family had dinner together and the father continued tenderly, to hold the baby.

In the third hour with us the child went quickly to the now-familiar dollhouse and arranged the furniture to her satisfaction. The togetherness theme took over with new and rising intensity. Methodically and soberly, the child placed father, mother, and three children in a bathtub together. She then removed the entire family to the roof and the father and mother and children were all sitting, one on top of the other, on top of the house. Then, suddenly, her play ended, she jumbled the furniture and the dolls and began a wild puppet play in which large animals bit each other viciously. The whale bit the crocodile, and the crocodile bit the giraffe. And then, finally, apparently carried away by her play, the child broke through the play and bit the crocodile savagely and then pummeled it out of shape. All of this, including her final giving way to anger, attack and loss of control, occurred in the total absence of any sound.

Wallerstein and Kelly walk us through the children's reactions through their developmental stages, providing equally affecting descriptions of little individuals through the years. The six- to eight-year-olds are described as bearing a great sadness and sense of loss, not evidenced in the younger ones. The nine- to twelve-year-olds were seen as having a much more layered response, but the predominant emotion expressed was anger. It is children in this age range who are most susceptible to efforts of one parent to create a wall of rejection against the other. It seems that these young people are more likely to be drawn into the divorce war, if the parents choose to engage in it. While the wounded spouse, suffering with overwhelming feelings of rejection and betrayal, might gain short-term satisfaction from their children's jumping on that particular bandwagon, the years of distress that follow are hardly worth the reward.

Co-parenting children after divorce is a challenge for even the least stressed parents. Almost always, children have a difficult time settling in to each parent's home after a transition. The more combative, least secure parents are quick to blame the other for the anxiety and acting out in the first day after the exchange. Thus, something altogether normal is transformed into grounds for battle. The same can be said of inherently challenging issues like when and how to introduce children to new partners; whether a child should receive medication or alternative treatment for ADHD; how to respond when children report unsavory behavior or hostile comments in the other parent's home; what to do if a child says they don't want to go to the other parent's home; or if the child doesn't like his step-siblings. The list can, of course, go on for pages. Certainly, if parents can address these difficult moments cooperatively with each other, the result will be much more supportive to children than if each is angry and blaming. Enlisting the assistance of an experienced, supportive professional is recommended when the inevitable speed bumps are encountered.

As observed by one pair of experienced co-parent counselors, "There's no such thing as a perfect family, a perfect childhood, or a perfect residential schedule. Our job, as co-parents, is to take an imperfect situation and smooth out the rough edges as best we can."[22]

Parents also need to realize that they are different people, each of whom provide valuable life lessons to their children. You might not like some of the qualities of your ex. She might be too uptight, even to the point of your labeling her OCD. He might be so lax that you wake up in the middle of the night with images of your four-year-old sticking a knife in the electrical socket. She might be loose as to time, sometimes arriving fifteen minutes late for the exchange, and in response you are furious at the insensitivity and irresponsibility. Many of the "complementary" qualities that both attracted and repelled each person as they moved down the path to divorce might rise in bold relief, now that children are involved. When anxiety and conflict are high, it is much harder to accept *the reality* that you are just different people, and the other person's qualities are unlikely to harm the children.

ATTACHMENT
AND
RESIDENTIAL ARRANGEMENTS FOR KIDS

Earlier, we discussed how *adult* attachment is at the heart of our intimate bonds—which helps explain the trauma of divorce for many of us. If we go back in time, though, we will also recall that attachment first described the relationship between an infant and his parent. At around eight months, this connection is completely dialed in, as evidenced by the baby's development of stranger anxiety. So, how does this play into discussions about residential arrangements for children? Funny you should ask. I was just about to talk about that.

A leading organization that focuses on post-divorce parenting is the Association of Family and Conciliation Courts. Their journal is called the *Family Court Review*, considered the gold standard in the field. A few years ago, the editors put a call out to the membership for feedback on the most important custody-related topics. Based on the responses, the issue of *attachment's role in custody decisions* was at the top of the list. So, in the summer of 2011, the *Family Court Review* put out an entire issue devoted to the topic.

One question that has perplexed people in the field is whether overnight stays with the non-primary caregiver is harmful for children up to a certain age. That age is most often set at three years old. So, for a considerable time, important voices in the field of children and divorce have discouraged such overnights for these little ones. This preference was stated, again, in some of the articles and interviews in the *Family Court Review*.

Two leading researchers in the field, Carol George and Judith Solomon, spoke about their work, which supported this limitation. As

George noted, "Overnights might work for some families, but many babies under a year-and-a-half or two seem to show that regular overnights away from their primary caregiver are stressful."

This seemingly simple prescription met with significant push-back in a subsequent issue. Studies and examples were cited, which were at odds with the Solomon and George conclusions. Maybe, experts thought, we need to step back from a hard and fast rule. Nonetheless, the Summer, 2011, issue shared a number of insights that are not at all controversial, such as:

- Fathers, as well as mothers, are attachment figures for babies. While mothers' roles include soothing the infant more than fathers, as a general rule, there is no evidence that fathers do not also provide this kind of nurturance as well.

- There is no correlation between an equal residential schedule and a father's ability to establish a strong attachment bond with his child. The advice of Alan Sroufe, an attachment expert, is, "Depending on your age, you will have the next 50 or 60 years for a relationship with this child. And they are going to need you all that time. You will not be displaced: attachment relationships aren't interchangeable.... If a stepparent comes along, they can also be a really useful figure in a child's life. But they will never replace that other parent." Most critical for a baby is frequent and consistent contact with *both* parents.

- If hostility and conflict between the parents results in a chronic state of fear and anxiety in either parent, particularly if it is the mother (if she is the primary caregiver for an infant), this will severely and negatively impact the child.

- Attachment, while significant, is only one factor to consider when constructing a residential schedule for a child younger than three years of age. Other critical considerations are: the nature of the relationship between the child and each parent prior to separation; the temperament of the child, including her ability to tolerate (or even flourish with) changes in overnight residence; the child's age and developmental level.

It is very difficult for a mother who has primarily cared for an infant to let go of that child and allow him to sleep at the other parent's home without experiencing a deep sense of loss and natural maternal anxiety. This needs to be honestly explored and not confused with a belief in what is in the best interests of the child.

Other experts on divorce and children have written volumes in recent years about fathers and divorce. Some feel that the legal system is unreasonably biased against fathers and the critical nature of their role in a child's life. Joan Kelly made this interesting observation in an article written in 2005:[23]

> *For reasons not entirely clear, the specific visiting pattern of every other weekend with the nonresidential parent, usually the father, became the favored and traditional arrangement for children following separation. This alternating weekend pattern may have gained favor because it was easy to apply, requiring no judicial or psychological analysis. It simply divided the child's leisure time during the school year between parents, assigning divorced mothers all the work of raising children, including discipline, homework, and childcare, and typically excluding fathers from these normal parenting responsibilities and opportunities.*

One of the shames of adversarial divorce is that "fathers' rights" and "mothers' rights" groups have sprung up around the country. The more politicized parenting becomes, the more we are distracted from understanding what children need.

The good news is that children *do* adjust to their parents' divorce if allowed to. Study after study over the past thirty years reveals that the overwhelming majority of children of divorce are resilient and by no means are "damaged" by their parents' divorce. Yet, to make that a reality, the parents must find an avenue for resolving the end of their marriage that will not traumatize their children. The key to this child-protective uncoupling is to understand that while your spousal relationship is ending, your parental (your *co-parental*) relationship continues. No two processes are more effective in achieving this result than mediation and collaborative divorce. It's time to explore these two avenues.

<u>TAKEAWAYS</u>

- While divorce is tough on children, it is unlikely to damage or cripple them. So, if reason exists for you to end the marriage, don't let the impact on your children stop you. If your partner ends the relationship, don't dwell on the trauma to your children caused by the "breakup of the family." They'll end up fine—as long as you find a way to manage your own life transition and don't project your anger, outrage, and loss onto them.

- Your kids are kids. Let them be kids. Join with your former partner in protecting them from your avoidable conflict.

- Get professional help to determine what conflict is avoidable and how to separate your children's best interests from your own best interests (or your view of their best interests through frightened and wounded eyes).

- Your children's well-being is closely tied to your well-being. You must take care of yourself. Always keep that in mind.

- Co-parenting is a job. It is a high calling requiring care and integrity. Strive for the personal qualities that will help you support and protect your children—NOT from the other parent, but from the uncertainty and challenges of this life transition.

CHAPTER 7

Doing Divorce Right
~ Mediation ~

A Note on Adam and Beth

In these last two chapters, our friends will be making two changes. In the first, they have entered a time machine. However, it is a technology in its infancy and can only move people back and forth one year at a time. (So no visiting the dinosaurs, the Last Supper, Babe Ruth's "called shot homerun," or your mom and dad's first date.) We will now revisit them before Beth had her first appointment with Linda, the divorce lawyer. Now Beth will choose, instead, to pursue a non-adversarial legal approach to resolving her divorce issues with Adam. The second change is that our friends have learned a little patience and have agreed to let their story be told later in the chapter, rather than at the beginning. So, as you read the following passages, imagine Beth meditating and Adam working with his therapist to cultivate forbearance. (But don't expect them to be mellow and all "Kumbaya" when we join them later for the negotiations on their legal divorce.)

THE ALTAR
OF SETTLEMENT

Mediation has been a significant part of the fabric of the divorce world for many decades. The underlying idea is simple: With the assistance of a *neutral* third person, people can arrive at their own solutions to their conflicts. After all, who do you want to come up with the best way to divide your marital assets/liabilities or figure out a residential schedule for your children—the two of you, or some third person who doesn't know anything about you? Well, that last part isn't true, they do know things about you, and those are the things that are force-fed the person in robes by lawyers in an adversarial dispute. So, really, they don't *know* you.

Mediation puts the lie to the belief that people in conflict need to turn to someone else to tell them what to do. Mediation tells you that you have the intelligence and inner resources to work with your estranged spouse to arrive at a set of solutions to your mutual problems. After all, if you agreed on something from the start, it wouldn't be a problem, would it? If you don't agree, even if one or both of you feel strongly about it, that doesn't mean you can't come to a solution yourselves. Now, to be sure, you might not be able to do it completely on your own, but with the assistance of somebody who, by training, experience, and temperament, can support and guide you through the process, you can, indeed, fashion your own solutions.

Participants in mediation have greater responsibility than those who use litigation to resolve their disputes. Here, you have to both speak so the other can understand your needs and interests, and you have to listen for the other person's message, as well. Speak and listen—that's the heart of mediation. Well, speak and listen and then work together to solve your joint problems. The key players in a mediated divorce are the two participants, the mediator, and the consulting lawyers who each work with one of the participants.

Remember the ad you saw on TV recently for some great diet program? I can guarantee that at the end, the voice coming out of your speaker said, "Check with your physician before starting on any new diet plan." It makes sense, because if you are going to do something that might affect your health and body, you ought to check with a professional that deals with health and the body. When the engine light flashes on your dashboard, I doubt that you ignore it and just drive on, blithely disregarding the growing noises coming from underneath your hood. Odds are that you haven't spent a lot of time learning how to service your own car, so you will take it to a person who does that for a living. You get the idea. So why wouldn't someone who is going to deal with something that affects their *legal* rights and responsibilities talk to a lawyer before they make these important decisions? Until the last few years, people avoided lawyers for two major reasons. First, lawyers are notorious for ramping up conflict. The worry is that a settlement agreement that works for both people will get blown up by the lawyer. "Don't agree to that! No judge would order that!" The second reason is that people are used to the idea of walking into a lawyer's office and paying $3,000; $5,000; $10,000; or more as a fee deposit (also called "a retainer"). While there are promises of a refund of any money left in the account when the work is done, full-on legal services are expensive, and people don't realistically expect to get any of that money back. For understandable reasons, people stayed away from lawyers in droves unless they had the money and wanted to duke it out over finances or kids.

"UNBUNDLING" LEGAL SERVICES
~MAKING LAWYERS ACCESSIBLE~

While lawyers may blanch at the idea, the development of unbundled legal services is an extension of the same movement that brought us technical support with Indian accents and rock-bottom Walmart wares. Say what you will about the inherent inequalities of the market economy (and there is much to say), it will always be an engine of innovation.

The legal economy has, for decades, excluded a large segment of our population, based on financial resources. In order to obtain the services of a lawyer, a prospective client was expected to make an enormous investment, in money, time, and trust. The attorney took a significant up-front deposit and handled the matter from start to finish, from soup to nuts, from Belgian clowns to…you catch my drift. Since divorce has been, *by far*, the most common court proceeding, many people who couldn't afford the entire breadth of services turned to self-help publications. Chief among these was *Nolo Press*, which published its first do-it-yourself legal guide, *How to Do Your Own Divorce in California* in 1971. *Nolo* is still going strong today.

The notion of "limited legal services" has been around for some time but has faced resistance from the legal community. One reason is the basic conservative nature of lawyers. That's conservative as in, "It's been done a certain way for a long time for a reason and there is no reason to change." Lawyers by training and predilection are wary of innovation, as a general rule.

This is not without cause. Who but a lawyer will be deeply aware of the risk of liability for a negative outcome when an individual who gets but a morsel of advice goes off on their own and makes a mistake that costs them dearly? Fair or not (usually unfair), this aggrieved person will look to the lawyer for compensation for the incomplete advice or service. Attorneys were understandably wary of taking that risk. This also reflected the natural complexity of every corner of life, once you get into it. From law to auto mechanics to football to mothering—you name it—everything has its multiple nooks and crannies of knowledge, folk wisdom, common problems, solutions, and unanticipated hazards. It seemed unfair to the uninitiated layperson to send them out with only part of the information they would need.

However, as the new century dawned, the legal establishment was rethinking its resistance to this notion. "Access to justice" became a catch phrase and driving force. Lawyers began to turn their considerable talents to finding a way to serve people who needed their services—just not *all* their services. This has led to the advent of "limited legal services." It is based in part on the dawning insight within the legal community that clients are adults and can make their own decisions. This is not to be snide. Over the last thirty years or so, "client autonomy" has forced itself to the top of the legal value pyramid. From a time in which lawyers knew best and gave advice from their own perspective, we are now well into the era in which it is recognized that individuals come to attorneys with a wide, complex, and often idiosyncratic array of interests based on their own history, current environment, and makeup. There has been a growing, and welcome, appreciation for the non-legal concerns that people bring with them to their legal disputes.

The response of the legal establishment is the evolution of *unbundled* legal services. The American Bar Association has developed an Unbundled Legal Services Resource Center. A Google search of the topic results in hundreds of hits. Hardly a community exists that doesn't have *some lawyer* who provides unbundled services.

The client will usually be asked to sign an agreement acknowledging their acceptance of the limited nature of the services being provided and assuming the risk of not having a lawyer at their elbow for the entire course of the matter. Once established, this relationship might be the most valuable asset a divorcing person has. Having a lawyer available to provide information and guidance during a process in which you will sit with your partner, the only professional support being the mediator before you, is the key to a thoughtful, equitable, satisfying, and durable mediated agreement.

WHAT IS MEDIATION?

Christopher W. Moore, an internationally recognized mediation trainer and author, describes mediation as,

> *...an intervention into a dispute or negotiation by an acceptable, impartial and neutral 3rd party who has no authoritative decision-making power, to assist disputing parties in voluntarily reaching their own mutually acceptable settlement of the issues in dispute.*

This passage describes the role of not just the divorce mediator. It is also the person who helps to resolve the battles between neighbors, labor and management, and nations. On the world stage, Theodore Roosevelt won the Nobel Peace Prize for his efforts to bring the Russian-Japanese war of the early 1900s to a close, and Jimmy Carter mediated a peace agreement between Israel and Egypt during his presidency. On a more personal, intimate stage, mediators have worked for decades with divorcing couples to achieve a mutually acceptable agreement. Whether it is Menachem Begin and Anwar Sadat or Bill and Mary Jones, the principles are the same.

Two sides enter mediation with differences that can range from slight to intense and entrenched. If the latter, there is still no reason the gulf can't be bridged. That is the professional work of a mediator, after all.

The first step is to provide a clear structure of the process. Sitting in the same room with the person who worries, hurts, and annoys you is a prospect few will relish. A major job of the mediator is to create a platform of safety for the participants. Without that, what's the point of putting yourself through the stress? The good mediator will have an intuitive feel for the temperature in the room, and at the outset will establish rules to control the communication and interaction. By doing this, the anxiety in the room will be lowered, and people can roll up their sleeves and get down to business.

Each person will be provided the time and space to talk about their view of the issue without fear of interruption. It is quite common that people in stressful conflict will hear the other say something and be compelled to cut in to set the record straight. "That's not true," or "That's not the whole story," they will want to say. The impulse to interrupt can be intense and constant. This won't be allowed to occur in a well-run mediation session. Everybody will have an opportunity to respond to what they believe to be errors or misstatements—just in their time. It is often said that the individuals in conflict "own" the issues and the resulting solution, but the mediator "owns" the process. The "roadmap" has to be made clear. Otherwise, mediation is nothing more than inviting a third voice into a dispute, and that can make the foundation very wobbly. As Moore says, mediation is *not* about a third person making a decision. That is what *arbitration* is. Also, it is not about the mediator siding with one person and persuading the other that he is wrong. The mediator must be neutral *and perceived by all involved parties as neutral*.

The next step is to begin to identify your needs, so you know what you're driving for. The skilled mediator will help each person identify and express their needs in a manner that the other can hear—and understand. This adage is key: my understanding you doesn't mean I agree with you or am willing to give up what I need. It's quite the opposite. In accomplishing this task, perhaps the mediator's most valuable tool is *the reframe*. This is the ability to "translate" what initially might be a harsh, confrontational, or positional statement so that its essence can be uncovered. After all, if I feel attacked by you, I will huddle. If I am hearing your expression of need, I may be inclined to have greater interest, especially if I am being afforded the same consideration.

"He's a bad father," can be reframed when the mediator says, "So you are concerned about the welfare of your children. Talk more about that." The discussion can then turn to mom's concerns about her children, rather than what's wrong with Dad. "She's not getting a penny of my pension," can be reframed when the mediator says, "You worked hard for that pension and you're worried about your financial well-being." The guy may respond, "No, that's not it at all. I have gotten no recognition for the sacrifices I made supporting her and the kids." It is almost a guarantee that he will not feel put off if the mediator's shot at understanding fails to be right on point. Almost always, there will be a correction, and the discussion will move on.

This highlights the two essential ingredients of what has come to be called *transformative mediation*. The first is *recognition*. I need to have my needs, concerns, and interests recognized by the other person in the dispute. That's different from needing them to agree with me. Being seen, knowing I have legitimacy in the other's eyes, is indispensable if we are to come to some accord. People in ragged conflict often complain that they are not "respected" by the other person. Again, this isn't because they are not agreed with. It is that they do not feel *seen*.

The second critical factor, *empowerment*, is illustrated by the following true story:[24]

At a professional training, a group of experienced mediators watched a role-play of a divorce mediation session in which the wife agreed to pay the husband far more than a court would have permitted and which the workshop participants believed was objectively unfair. There was absolutely no evidence of coercion or the failure of the wife to completely understand what she was doing and the options available to her. Following the demonstration, the room erupted with denunciations about what the mediator had allowed. Virtually all the voices were raised to provide concrete suggestions for what might have been said by the mediator to avoid this train wreck. For many years, mediation as practiced by a wide swath of the community assumed that the professional knew what was best for the participants and should actively work to prevent an outcome that was considered, not by the participants, *but by the mediator* to be unfair or aberrant. Client empowerment, or autonomy, in making their own decisions was beside the point. Thankfully, no longer. Mediation, as currently practiced by the vast majority of experienced practitioners, now provides this autonomy to the individuals involved. The professionals' job is to ensure that all decisions are made knowingly, thoughtfully, and not as a result of coercion. Yet, within these boundaries, they must be the decisions of the involved parties.

In some respects, mediators perform similar functions to therapists. They create an environment of safety. They reframe statements in a way that permits the other person to understand the underlying needs expressed, without feeling attacked. They establish a structured process, within which each person can express their concerns. The major difference (and it is a *major* difference) is that mediators are specifically goal-oriented. People come to a mediator because they have conflict over a certain set of issues, and the mediator helps them *come to agreement* about these issues.

A mediation session can last anywhere from a couple of hours to a whole day. There can be a single meeting or a series of meetings, depending on the needs of the participants and the style of the mediator. While the longer meetings might seem more efficient, people's capacity to process information and work with each other deteriorates over time. After about two hours, there is usually a steep drop-off in productivity. Unless there is a concern about safety or intimidation (which needs to be explored at the outset of the process), people will sit together in the same room. Often, they will sit at the same side of the table rather than across from one another. That has been described as a graphic depiction of the fact that the parties don't look to each other as the problem, but are on the same side and the problem is on the other side. It has often been said in my office, "Solving Sue's problem is not just Sue's job, it's Bob and Sue's job. Solving Bob's problem isn't just Bob's job. It's Sue and Bob's job." (That has been especially effective when the client's names are Bob and Sue!)

A good mediator makes sure that both people have the support they need. Very often, one partner is more experienced and sophisticated about financial issues, and that will make the other uneasy—understandably so. Nobody should go through a mediation process without being 100% comfortable that they understand what is going on. Both people should get the support of a lawyer. That is where unbundled legal services come in.

Another of the keystones of a successful mediation process is "transparency." This means that both people provide all the information the other needs in order to make informed decisions about the topic under discussion. A lawyer who is supportive of the settlement process can be extremely helpful in advising you what information you will need. In my experience, lawyers who litigate for a living tend to "over-ask," seeking a mountain of unnecessary information, thereby making the process much more burdensome than it needs to be. An experienced lawyer can glean a lot of valuable information from tax returns, credit card statements, and bank records. Few people really attempt to hide assets (and the vast majority of those who try, fail).

Broadly speaking, there are two kinds of mediation that people who are divorcing will use. There is *"evaluative"* mediation, and there is *"facilitative"* mediation. In the first, a retired judge or experienced divorce lawyer will tell the parties what is likely to happen in court. That will be the only real basis for decision. In facilitative mediation, the needs that each person brings with them into the process are expressed and explored with the goal of satisfying the reachable needs of each. The approach described here is much more *facilitative* or *transformative* than *evaluative*.

THE SHADOW OF THE LAW
AND
THE CULTURE OF THE MARRIAGE

The goal in settling a divorce, whether by way of mediation or the collaborative law process (see next chapter), is to arrive at a *Durable Agreement*. This can be described as an agreement that both people can accept without anger or resentment. It is an agreement that responds to the reachable needs of each person and results from a process where each person honestly felt *heard* and *respected*. Both people are satisfied with a durable agreement when they sign it, the next morning, six months later, and five years later. The individuals have had a chance to sleep on it before committing themselves, and all questions have been answered. This is a far cry from the conventional settlement conference described in an earlier section, in which an entire day is spent working toward a settlement, and that is the one and only goal—getting something signed by the end of the day. There's *lots* of morning-after misgivings with these. Conventional lawyer thinking is that if we give people time to ruminate about the deal they made, each will re-think and move away from the deal, so you'd better get them locked in now or else the agreement will be lost. That philosophy seems to define a *non*-durable agreement, since it is expected that people will have doubts and objections after they have thought about it…but it's too late. Bear in mind, lawyers make it crystal clear to people signing these agreements that they are binding themselves and can't come back later and try to undo it. That doesn't mean they'll be happy with it— probably not if there is any sense of pressure or exhaustion when these agreements are signed.

So if the goal is a Durable Agreement, the obvious questions are, "What are its elements? What do you need in order to get one?" The answers are simple. Only two elements support such an agreement, as far as I can see. The first is what I call "the shadow of the law." This excellent phrase was coined over thirty years ago in the *Yale Law Journal*'s "Bargaining in the Shadow of the Law," an article describing divorce mediation. Laws reflect the basic values and culture of a particular society. Each state has its own set of divorce laws. Agreements need to be entered into with an understanding of the values that are reflected in these laws, but not necessarily be slavishly consistent with them.

The other critical element may be described as the "culture of the marriage." What did the people talk about and think was important? What are the values of these two people and what will work for them? An excellent example is shared by New York family lawyer and mediator Barry Berkman on an episode of *This American Life*, a popular public radio program. A man and woman who were divorcing had small children they were both deeply committed to parenting. They were excellent co-parents, and they had decided that the best plan was for them to live close together, which would facilitate the cooperative parenting they and their children wanted. She had a lot of her own family money. He did not, and his income was fairly meager, as he made his living as a musician. They agreed that she would purchase for him a co-op unit close to her home. They were both quite satisfied with that solution, and each went to their own lawyers to get final advice on wording their agreement. When her lawyer reviewed the agreement, the immediate question was, basically, "Why are you doing this? No court would order you to give him anything close to this." She was strongly dissuaded from making such an agreement. She backed out. They proceeded to acrimonious litigation in which claims of inappropriate parenting decisions were lobbed back and forth, forever poisoning the relationship. In this case, the *culture of the marriage* was given exactly zero weight.

There must be a balance between these two elements—the *shadow of the law* and the *culture of the marriage*—in order for an agreement to have a strong foundation and to endure.

ANOTHER LOOK AT "CONFLICT"

Mediators understand that conflict is not a horrible failure—a monster to be avoided. To be sure, conflict for some of us can shake loose the oldest ghosts rattling deep inside of us. Yet, for most of us, conflict is just hard and painful. Intimate conflict is more painful still. Conflict after the rupture of an intimate bond is even more painful. Through all of this, mediators know that conflict is nothing if not normal. The existence of conflict *certainly* doesn't mean that true resolution and peace cannot be achieved. This is particularly important to understand if passions are intense and the stakes feel high. Mediators know that conflict over "principle" (which is hard to resolve) can be shifted to conflict over divisible interests (which are manageable); conflict over a "zero sum" pot, in which one person's gain is another's loss (hard to resolve) can be shifted to an expanded pie, which allows each person to satisfy their interests without diminishing the other's (manageable); conflict between parties who will have no further interaction is harder to resolve than conflict between those who will have continued contact and interaction (and interdependence) well into the future (how better to describe the relationship of people divorcing with children?); conflict over one global issue (harder to resolve) can be shifted to conflict over a series of smaller issues (manageable); and conflict over a permanent potential outcome (hard) can be shifted to conflict over progressive and temporary outcomes (manageable).

Adam and Beth

Beth had received the name of a mediator from her therapist, Delores. She had emailed Adam, saying that she wanted him to consider this option. She desperately wanted to avoid court. Beth had heard too many horror stories from friends and family members and didn't want to subject Jason and Lilly to what she had seen when the parents of Jason's friend Ben (and also good friends of theirs) had split up. It had been extremely ugly. She and Adam had felt pressured to choose sides and, eventually, both of these old friends had drifted away. When she had searched for divorce lawyers on the web, Beth became dispirited, and when she told this to Delores, she received the referral to Mel. She spoke with him on the phone, and he had carefully explained his approach, which sounded right for them. Mel had asked that she have Adam call him, too, so he could explain everything to her husband as well. When Beth started to tell Mel that her real worry was that Adam would push for 50/50 time with the kids, when he had been such a workaholic during the marriage, Mel had gently stopped her, saying, "I know this concerns you, Beth, but I ask everyone I speak with in this initial conversation to not talk with me about the substance of your concerns, without the other person being part of the conversation. I have found that the most important thing I can offer, besides my experience, is my neutrality—but it's not just that. It's also people's *trust* in my neutrality. If Adam worries that you have told me something at the beginning that might make me more sympathetic to you, or if you worry that Adam has told me something that might make me more sympathetic to him, then that basic trust in my neutrality will be damaged. If that happens, I won't be able to help you both. That's why I like to have these discussions when we are all together." That made sense to her, and she liked the way Mel had explained it.

So now she and Adam sat in Mel's waiting room. He had told them there were no records or documents they needed to bring to the first meeting. They just needed to bring themselves. Beth was worried about money. Well, that wasn't quite right. She was worried about money and the children. Beth had loved being a mother, from the smell of baby powder on Lilly's chubby body all the way to nudging Jason about finishing his homework before he jumped on his computer. Jason was pretty good at it on his own, but still, she had to inject her maternal sternness once in a while. Lilly was full-on into adolescence. She was going to need her mother a lot for the next few years. She couldn't imagine the kids being at Adam's house on weekends. The idea that they would be away from her half the time, like he had said he wanted in his latest email to her, was inconceivable. She didn't think there was any reason to talk about another subject if he was stubborn about that. She had decided to make that clear from the very beginning. Then there was the money. How was she going to live? She hadn't been in the work force in thirteen years. She had been a pharmaceutical rep, having gotten the job from a connection Adam had. Beth had done well, but quit after only two years when Lilly arrived. She hoped she could get Mel to convince Adam that splitting his income with her for the next five years, plus paying for her to go back to school to get a counseling degree (so she could work with kids) was fair. She was relying on Mel for this. Daisy had told her that a close mutual friend had gotten more than that in her divorce. While Beth wanted to work this out without going to court, if Adam wasn't willing to be reasonable, then she would take it to a judge. She hoped that, with Mel's help, Adam would understand she was dead serious.

Adam sat beside Beth in Mel's waiting room and, smelling her familiar perfume, was thinking how good she looked today. Of course, he was with Susie now, but he always found Beth hot, even when he wasn't getting along with her. He wondered if she had worn the perfume just to throw him off his game. He and Susie had talked about the mediation until midnight and he was ready for whatever Beth threw at him. All he knew was that he was going to be taking care of Lilly and Jason for years to come—covering their college expenses and such—but he felt differently about his wife. Beth was an adult and had been successful in her pharmaceutical rep job. She was smart and attractive, and if she would stop being so full of doubt and negativity, she'd have a great job in no time. Adam felt his palms sweating and wiped them hard on the knees of his khakis just as the door to Mel's office opened, and he emerged with an easy smile on his face.

All Mel knew about Adam and Beth was that they had been married for fifteen years, had two teenaged children, Adam worked and Beth did not, and they were getting divorced. He noted as he welcomed them into his office that each was casually but appropriately dressed and each had a laptop. Mel had mixed feelings about three laptops opened on the table—barriers all around—but decided to let it go at the beginning and see if it impeded the task of helping these people formulate and express their concerns and interests. He usually started with a ten-minute introduction, which included a review and signing of the brief mediation agreement. He found that sitting and listening to him for a bit drained off some of the nervous energy. He wanted to make sure that each felt safe, so he emphasized the communication ground rules and got the commitment from each that his interceding if emotions led to destructive interaction would be acceptable. Mel then told them he wanted to know what their greatest needs and concerns were and waited to see who spoke first.

Adam had worked this out the night before and felt confident about what he wanted to say, so he jumped into the breach. "I think it's important to understand that it is Beth who walked away from this marriage. It was her choice and..." Mel looked over to Beth and saw that she had turned her head away from Adam, and the muscles in her jaw were working. "... I don't think it's fair that she gets to walk away and take my kids and take my money. I love my kids. I'm their father and there is no reason that I shouldn't have them 50/50." Beth couldn't help herself, saying, "That is wrong, Adam, and you know it." It had taken all her self-control not to yell, "Bullshit!" to this ridiculous notion, but she could certainly say, "That's ridiculous. Who is Lilly's new best friend? How does her math tutor say she is doing? You haven't a clue." Adam was about to respond when Mel interjected, "Look, it is completely understandable that each of you is going to have strong feelings about what the other says, and there is going to be this overwhelming urge to speak up and set the record straight or correct inaccuracies you hear. I'm going to ask each of you to take a deep breath when the other is speaking, and use the pad and pen in front of you to take notes. When it is your turn to speak, you can say what you need to. If I allow each of you to interrupt the other when you feel a burning need, then it will happen all day, and this won't be a safe *or* useful process for you. Is that all right with you both?" Mel could see both Adam and Beth visibly relax and readily assent when he was finished. He had taken control of the process and begun to construct an environment in which conflict resolution could occur.

Adam continued by saying that he had concerns that Beth had developed a drinking problem and he didn't think the kids were safe with her once she had opened a bottle of wine at night. (Adam *did* have concerns, but he also wanted Beth to know that he would use her drinking if she wanted to fight him over the kids.) Mel stopped Adam and asked him if he could just get some clarification about his concerns. Careful probing by Mel revealed that Adam had never experienced a drinking "problem" with Beth until they had separated, and he based his concern mostly on the number of bottles (four) in the recycle bin when he recently came to the house to pick up the kids. He and Beth had engaged in a particularly unpleasant telephone conversation, when the kids had been with him and watching a movie, and Beth had clearly been inebriated. Mel asked Adam if he had ever experienced Beth do anything with the kids that bothered him when they were with her. He conceded that he had not, but insisted that he worried about alcohol. Mel had responded, simply, "So, Adam, you just want to make sure that Beth knows your concerns and can assure you that she won't drink to excess when Lilly and Jason are with her." Adam couldn't do anything other than agree to that statement. Then Mel turned to Beth and said, "Beth, setting aside, for the moment, your feelings about Adam's raising this issue at the outset, are you comfortable with the basic notion of assuring him that you won't be drinking to excess while the children are residing with you?" While still irritated at the way Adam had started out, she responded quickly, a bit self-righteously, "Absolutely." "Wonderful," Mel had said with a smile. "Your first agreement." (To be sure, issues of substance abuse might often be more vexing than what Adam and Beth present. Yet, this challenge may often be met effectively by reframing the issue as, not one of one person's blameworthy behavior, but rather, how this behavior causes anxiety with the other person. Mediators can effectively leverage a person's declared interest in arriving at a mutually agreeable outcome by getting the suspected substance abusing partner to agree to an evaluation with a person chosen by the mediator and vetted by each person so that this issue, which is obviously causing considerable unease between the partners, can be addressed and resolved.)

Even though it seemed like the smallest of accomplishments, given the tense and hurt feelings that still hovered between them like a pall of stale cigarette smoke, Mel's comment was the first of many that began to create an edifice of small agreements. Mel knew that the bigger issues, like the children's residential plan and how to reach agreement on support for Beth, were still a meeting (or two…or three) away, but one tried and true rule of divorce mediation is that you get agreement on the less difficult issues early, if you can, so that a spirit of cooperation begins to seep into the process.

Adam and Beth seemed to get locked up in the discussion about maintenance for Beth and her desire to get retrained. Adam said more than a few times that he couldn't see why he had to support Beth after *she* had walked out of the marriage. This is where a little education and perspective-taking from Mel helped. On the education side, Mel reminded them that the end of a marriage almost always came when both people were unable to make the relationship work. "It's not so much about blame," Mel said. "It's more about how a marriage can erode over time until usually one person says they can't do it anymore. For the one who is 'left,' it feels very painful, but, in my experience, a person's not the 'bad guy' for deciding to end the marriage. It's more in how they do it. There's a really good book out there by Joseph Shaub that explains the process well. I recommend it to you both." On the perspective-taking side, Mel got them to re-confirm that they wanted the best outcome for their children. When Adam had taken a shot at Beth by commenting that, "Divorce is *always* a horrible outcome for children," Mel had intervened, noting that children generally do fine after their parents' divorce, so long as they are not exposed to parental conflict. He added that their decision to enter a mediation process was an excellent indication that they placed their children's best interests at the top of their value scale. In order for them to continue this, it was going to be important that Beth find a path to self-sufficiency and a sense of meaning in her work, "just as you have enjoyed over the years, Adam." Mel then ventured his own opinion: "Both of you have some responsibility as far as maintenance is concerned. Adam, you have some responsibility to give your wife a cushion that will allow her to make a transition to self-support and well-being. That will definitely serve you both in the future and particularly serve you, Adam, as the mother of your children will be secure and fulfilled and your financial obligations to her will be lessened after a time. Beth, your obligation is to think carefully about what you want to do and find out the various paths to get there. You need to be realistic about expense and time—it doesn't make sense, for example, for you to decide, 'I've always wanted to be a veterinarian, but I'll have to go back and take two years of prerequisites before I apply to vet school. Does that sound o.k. to both of you?' Beth had responded that she was working on her plans, and they were nothing like that. She also committed to sharing concrete details of her ideas with Mel and Adam three days before the next meeting so they could be discussed then. Both felt their basic interests had been addressed. Mel also made a point every time he imparted information or a viewpoint to check in with them to make sure they understood and were on board—and, if not, he was completely open to their questions and resistance.

The problem of a residential schedule for the children was rather more difficult. Adam had gotten himself dug in around 50/50, and the mediation had almost ended before it started when Beth had demanded that he concede that this was not going to happen before she agreed to proceed further. Mel had quickly interceded by acknowledging that this was clearly an important and emotional issue for them both *and* they needed a bit of time in the process before they could discuss it. Mel assured them that he had worked with many couples with a deadlock at the beginning of mediation, but, with a little patience and good will, they would be able to successfully work together to solve this problem in coming sessions. Mel was careful to describe this as a *mutual* problem for them *both* to solve.

When the time came to finally address parenting in a later session, Mel started on a positive note, commenting that it was good they had been separated for three months already, because they had worked out a tentative parenting schedule, without the help of a third person. They immediately disabused him of that notion. Beth said that the kids were with Adam every other weekend because they needed to stay in the house for less disruption. Adam said he had agreed to this as an interim measure. He now wanted 50/50 time. Mel immediately acknowledged their objections to his initial speculation and turned the subject to the children. How were Lilly and Jason doing? What were they like as individuals? Were they handling the divorce well, poorly…differently? The subject of Susie had been raised in the first session, so Mel was comfortable asking if the kids had met Susie. He approached this potentially volatile subject in a matter-of-fact way, trying to bleed out some of the topic's pressure. When Beth expressed outrage about Adam's relationship with Susie, and Adam shot back that it was Beth who threw him out, Mel observed that this was a sensitive topic for *each* of them. He promised to be as sensitive as he could be in discussing it, but he hoped they understood that it had to be discussed *and resolved* to the satisfaction of each of them. "The divorce is not going to *not* happen, and Susie is not going away, so we need to figure out together a residential schedule that works best for the children."

There had been discussions about how to talk to the children and how Beth and Adam would discuss Susie with (and in front of) the children. Mel warned Adam that the kids might have a negative reaction to Susie, and he said they hadn't so far. Mel asked if the children knew that he and Susie were together and planning on living together. Adam said, "Not yet." Mel responded, "Well, that's something we're going to need to discuss so we can come up with a solution that works for both of you and your kids." Surprisingly, Beth had come to the next session with some good ideas about how they could talk about Susie's inevitable future involvement in Lilly and Jason's lives. Still, the residential schedule felt like a very tough nut to crack. Mel eventually helped them resolve the deadlock by shifting the discussion from a long-term residential plan to a short-term plan. He told Adam and Beth that one of the advantages of a mediated parenting plan over one that is imposed by a judge (often after an exhaustive and exhausting evaluation and report by a psychologist) is that it is difficult to make any changes to a judge's final parenting arrangement. Lawyers and judges strive for stability and consistency, so the idea of changing a parenting plan is discouraged. However, if people agree to a mediation process, where they can discuss any changes with the help of a third person, it is much more likely that they can make solid, yet flexible, plans for the children. Mel said, "You *could* come up with a plan that seems acceptable in the present to you for purposes of seeing how it works out." After having mulled on Adam's demand for 50/50 for a couple of months now, Beth had concluded that the biggest shortcoming was that Adam worked too hard to pull this off. Plus, Lilly said she knew that "Daddy is dating Susie," and she was resisting residential time with him. Mel suggested that they try a plan in which the children spent alternate, long weekends with Adam, from Thursday at the end of school to Monday's return to school. They could see how this worked for everyone and meet again in three months to reassess. When Beth said she'd be open to a discussion about extending Adam's time, if he would be willing to commit to not having Susie stay over with the kids there until they had discussed it all the way through, they came to a temporary agreement.

They worked out a temporary financial plan, with a surprising absence of difficulty. Mel wrote up the temporary agreements, and Beth and Adam brought them to their lawyers for review. Each lawyer suggested a couple of "tweaks," but these were settlement-friendly lawyers who provided unbundled legal services, and the first phase of mediation concluded successfully after four meetings.

MEDIATION ISN'T JUST ABOUT STAYING OUT OF COURT

The process described above is *not easy*. People who have strong feelings about the other and their history (and their future) must sit in the same room with each other, communicate, and make agreements. This is a challenge and requires the ability to tolerate this stress. Many people are capable of this and, in my view, ought to be given the chance. In conventional lawyers' thinking, each person needs to be "protected," and misgivings about having them negotiate on their own are robust, to put it mildly. Yet, along with the high expectations are significant rewards. The ability to speak your truth in a way that the other can hear (albeit with help); the opportunity to work together to fashion a resolution of your disagreements that respects the needs of each person to the extent feasible; and the creation of a platform to work through difficulties when emotions are charged, describe the greatest benefits of the mediation process.

Another major advantage of mediation is the cost, as no other process offers solid professional support at lower cost. However, the people who are struggling emotionally need to deal with each other alone (with the help of a single professional), without the buffer of lawyers or the sensed safety provided by separation into different rooms. Many people can do this. Individuals (or couples) who wrestle with power imbalances, or for whom the wounds of separation are too great, might not be able to deal with each other (with so much at stake) absent significantly greater support. As we have seen in earlier chapters, divorce *is*, at heart, an attachment injury, and it is not a failure or sign of personal weakness if one feels overwhelmed by the process. There *is* a lot going on, after all. In these cases, mediation might not be an experience that one or both people can tolerate. Yet, rather than abandon a process of facilitated settlement altogether (and hire conventional lawyers), these people might be exceedingly well-served to engage the collaborative divorce process. That will be the topic of the next chapter.

TAKEAWAYS

- **Mediation is the least expensive divorce process in which you can obtain the support and guidance of professionals. As such, it requires the most of the participants.**
- **Make a list of those factors that cause you to worry about whether mediation is right for you and your relationship. Be sure to explore these concerns with any mediator you consider engaging.**
- **Do not engage in mediation without obtaining unbundled support from an attorney.**
- **<u>Find a lawyer who is supportive of the settlement process!</u> This lawyer must understand not only the "shadow of the law" but also be mindful of the "culture of the relationship" and the possibility of outcomes that, knowingly made, might not reflect what a judge would order.**

CHAPTER 8

Doing Divorce Right
~ Collaborative Law ~

Given the fact that Collaborative Law has been with us for more than twenty-five years and boasts legions of committed practitioners in every state, it is a wonder that it is still unknown to many among us. It is a powerful approach to achieving a healthy divorce, as well as being a window into a creative and enthusiastic world of helping professionals who are focused on the well-being of the people they serve.

THE BEGINNING OF COLLABORATIVE LAW

It was the early '90s and Minneapolis family lawyer Stu Webb was deeply disenchanted. He was at the top of his game, a successful and well-respected member of the legal community. Stu had been Number One in his law school class. He'd worked in the divorce field for many years, and he was burned out. The negativity and poison of conventional legal battles over money, kids, security, revenge, outrage, and escalating conflict had brought him to say, "Enough." He was even thinking of leaving the field, altogether.

Then an idea entered his head that generations of lawyers since have found either ridiculous or inspired. "What if we could somehow agree to work out all the people's disputes without going to court?" A litigation-free divorce—now *there* was a wild concept. What were the chances that lawyers, born and bred in the Land of Litigation, would agree to such an outlandish idea? Well, you don't know until you try. So Stu reached out to the lawyers in his community and basically said, "Will you join me in working on divorce cases together in which we all agree not to go to court?"

Predictably, most of the other lawyers declined the invitation. I mean, how can you get someone in a legal proceeding to settle if they don't have the hammer of a potential negative judge's ruling hanging over their head? Yet, a handful of colleagues were of similar mind and chose to join Stu in finding a way to get this done. While it's all well and good to say you want to do something new and unconventional, how do you actually carry it out? Thus was born Collaborative Practice and the Participation Agreement.

They came up with the radical idea that the two divorcing people and their lawyers would all sign a contract stating that nobody would go to court in an adversarial proceeding. Everything would be decided by the divorcing people themselves. So that this commitment would mean something, everyone *also* agreed that if either person *did* go to court to get a judge to decide something for them, then both lawyers would withdraw and the individuals would have to hire new litigation counsel. Thus, a legal process was created, with the active participation of lawyers, where everyone committed *not to go to court.*

Think of the Great Plains in the middle of the country in the midst of a long drought—mile upon mile of parched grassland on a hot, dry, and windy day. Somebody touches a dry tuft with a match and "*Woompf,*" a fire erupts and spreads with rapidity and power. That was the impact of Stu Webb's idea. Almost immediately, family lawyers in the San Francisco Bay Area, the Midwest, New England, and Canada embraced this new model. A professional organization arose, the *International Academy of Collaborative Professionals (IACP),* which now boasts a membership of thousands of attorneys, therapists, and financial experts around the world. These people are all committed to exploring and refining this truly revolutionary approach to conflict resolution in divorce. (See *www.collaborativepractice.com.)*

Throughout the 1990s and beyond, a multitude of lawyers throughout the U.S., Australia, Canada, and Europe, hungry for a way to support divorcing people that was not destructive and toxic, rallied to Collaborative Practice. Early champions and trainers, like Pauline Tesler of California, warned lawyers that they would have to make a "paradigm shift" in order for this approach to work. For as much as lawyers wished to experience a healthier form of practice, old habits die hard. Any outcome that would leave anything on the table for the other spouse, beyond what a court would require, gave a lot of lawyers the heebie-jeebies. Disconnecting from a slavish commitment to outcomes that have to be in line with what a court would do is painful for many lawyers. Having consideration for interests other than those of their client can be a deeply disconcerting—even disorienting— notion. However, to varying degrees, lawyers are making this shift.

So this Collaborative Divorce idea was intriguing from the start— but no one said it was going to be easy. What professionals found quite frequently was that the clients who were being drawn to collaborative practice had a variety of motivations, some of which weren't conducive to achieving a positive outcome through a productive process. Some people thought it was a cheap way to get divorced. Some people just wanted to stay out of court, but they didn't want to give up their desire for "justice," as *they* understood that term. It became very clear that just signing an agreement to engage in a collaborative process did not mean that people were leaving their sense of outrage, umbrage, and panic at the door. "How to make it easier?" people in the field began to ask. They came upon the next innovation (after the truly remarkable notion of an agreement that the lawyers would withdraw if one of the people went to court). That step was *The Collaborative Team.*

There are a number of things that get shaken up when people are ending an intimate relationship or marriage. First, there are the obvious emotional issues. Divorce rocks your world. You've got to be able to work with, to negotiate with, and parent with the person who did the rocking. If we think our partner pushes our buttons when we're *together*, how do you think they will impact us when we are split up, our marriage reduced to spent embers? Getting help with lowering the emotional reactivity and finding tools for communication and conflict resolution are indispensable parts of a healthy divorce. Second, what about the kids? Far and away, the biggest complaint young adults have about their parents' divorce when they were children is that nobody talked to them. Plans were made for them—their lives were dramatically altered—and nobody ever asked them for any input. Also, adults get confused about parenting sometimes when divorce is happening. I have seen many committed, deeply loving parents talk about their children's best interests when it was quite clear that they were having a hard time unhooking this from their own best interests. If another person who was a professional dealing with the impact of divorce on kids were able to help the parents understand what their children were going through, it would be a much less lacerating experience for the younger ones. Finally, in order for people to make the important financial decisions that would guide the rest of their lives, both must understand the extent of their assets *and liabilities*, and appreciate that there are a number of ways to solve their money concerns in the wake of divorce. Enlisting a neutral financial expert who can create a clear picture of what's there (and what isn't), as well as encourage discussions about various strategies for solving current and future financial problems, is a wise and economical solution.

Thus was born the *collaborative team*. This team consists of the two lawyers, one or two mental health professional coaches, a financial specialist, and a child specialist. Many collaborative communities throughout the country decided not to even attempt a collaborative divorce unless a full team had been assembled. In some parts of the country, each person would have their own mental health professional "coach," and, in others, a couple would have one "coach" sit with them both together and help them. (Seasoned couples therapists are quite skilled at working with two people in conflict so that neither feels marginalized or excluded.) Terms like "container" were employed to describe the support that was being created for people during their challenging transition.

The collaborative divorce approach should *not* be chosen over litigation because it will save money. While it is somewhat less expensive, the real value is the *kind* of divorce process you have, not its cost. There is a whole different way of *thinking* for professionals who adopt this challenging and transformative approach to helping people uncouple. This shift is reflected not only in the way people conceive of their work, but also in their manner of talking.

The communication that transpires between the professionals on this team is far different than that which you'll see in conventional divorce. Let's say William represents Jane, a stay-at-home mother of three kids, now eight, twelve, and fifteen; and Helen represents Bart, a solo lawyer who's had his own practice for twenty years and takes home about $180,000 per year from his practice. He works hard, often losing evenings and weekends to his work. What might the first telephone conversation between William and Helen sound like in the conventional divorce?

William: Good afternoon, Helen. I just got retained by Jane Philips in her divorce and I'd like to talk to you about some interim arrangements.

Helen: Nice to hear from you, William. I look forward to working with you again. Yes, I've talked to Bart and we'd like to get something worked out.

W: Well, you know, Jane hasn't worked in years and she's the primary caretaker of the kids. She'll need some temporary alimony and, of course, the kids will be staying with her in the house for the time being.

H: That's not what I heard from my client. He said that Jane has an inheritance from her mother that's sitting in a money market account worth $500,000, and Bart's practice is in a long-term down cycle. His receivables have been in the neighborhood of $5,000 per month for the last 6 months, and he can barely afford an apartment big enough for his kids. He was also thinking that since he has his own practice, he's got some flexibility and wants to have 50/50 custody of the kids.

W: Well that's a non-starter for Jane. He can't suddenly decide that just because he's getting divorced he can cut his work hours back and lower his income and...

H: I assure you that's not what he's doing.

W: Please don't interrupt me...and the idea of 50/50 is, frankly, out of the question.

H: I suggest you talk to your client about her boyfriend coming around all the time and the damage that's doing to the children.

W: That has nothing at all to do with your client's work habits, and there's no way her new friend will have anything to do with the custody issue since he has been keeping his distance. The children only know him as "Bill, Mommy's friend," and that's it.

H: Okay, then, thank you for your insights. Should we set a date for a hearing, since it looks like we may not be able to see eye-to-eye on this?

W: That's a good idea. If you want to send me an interim settlement proposal, I'll be happy to forward it along to my client.

H: It'll be in my papers. I'll get them over to you by next Friday.

W: Thanks. Say "hello" to John for me.

H: Will do. Give my best to Katie.

This is an example of the professional and respectful discussions that occur thousands of times a day between divorce lawyers throughout the country. (While there are certainly loads of examples of edgy, unpleasant exchanges, as well, they are in the distinct minority.) While each lawyer may honestly believe he or she is projecting and protecting the interests of their client, they have set themselves up for an adversarial hearing in which each client's fears and concerns will hardly be considered in the courtroom (and in the resulting court order). How might a similar conversation occur between two collaborative lawyers?

William: Good afternoon, Helen. I just got retained by Jane Philips in her divorce and I'd like to talk to you about some interim arrangements.

Helen: Nice to hear from you, William. I look forward to working with you again. Yes, I've talked to Bart and we'd like to get something worked out.

W: Jane and I have a number of open dates in a couple of weeks for our first four-way meeting.

H: Great. Email them to me, and I'll pass them along to Bart and we'll get something on the calendar. Is there anything pressing that needs to be addressed before our meeting?

W: No emergencies. Jane is having a hard time living under the same roof as Bart. Things are getting tense around there, and I'd like to see how we can help them separate as soon as possible.

H: Jane may have told you this already, William, but Bart has had a down few months. I think it's partly the ups and downs of private practice, but also the fact he's been struggling with the marriage blowing up and Jane's new relationship. I don't think he can afford to cover the house expenses and move out. I understand that we do have some possible resources in Jane's inheritance.

W: Well, I think she'd be awful uncomfortable using her inheritance, which is her security, to pay her living expenses. That's definitely something we can discuss. Maybe they can agree to some reimbursement scheme or a cap on the use of her inheritance. I'll talk to Jane about the new relationship and see how she feels about making this a non-issue during the course of the divorce process. Maybe limit her contact. I'll see where she's at with that question. What's the chance of our getting business and personal bank records over the past three years?

H: I'll talk to Bart about that. I don't see that as a problem. We'll also need to start thinking about what Jane can do to move toward self-sufficiency. Maybe a vocational counselor? By the way, are things so tense in the house that we need to set up our first meeting sooner rather than later?

W: No, I think a couple or three weeks out will be okay. Look forward to seeing you then. Please call me or email me if you have any concerns before our meeting.

W: Okay. Talk to you soon.

What jumps out at you when you compare these two dialogues?

I have always thought of collaborative legal practice as a combination of promoting a client's interests while at the same time acknowledging the concerns of the other person. In a conventional divorce, it is more likely that Bart would try to make a case for a long-term, or permanent, downturn in his practice in order to pay less child support and alimony. He might even try to push for Jane getting a job doing anything now, regardless of the meagerness of her income and future prospects. Jane would erect a brick wall a mile high and a mile thick around her inheritance, claiming it is her separate, non-divisible property (which it is in every state's laws *I'm* aware of) and should not be considered in this divorce. She'll look back at the excellent income he enjoyed only three years ago and try to hold him to that level for purposes of setting any support. Bart is angry and feels that Jane blew up the marriage with her affair. Why does *he* have to move out of the house?

A collaborative approach, by contrast, might acknowledge that Jane and Bart living under the same roof is going to be hard on everyone, and lawyers and clients need to roll up their sleeves to figure out how they can manage this transition. Also, in the short term, Bart might have a greater financial obligation to Jane if she needs some education or training in order to shift into a career. How she thinks of her inheritance is an important area of discussion with a lot of angles. She's getting divorced, and that is a life circumstance that an inheritance might help with. If she needs to get some training or education, this might be a useful employment of the inheritance, in part—"in part" because a substantial portion of it needs to be preserved, since this might well be a good part of her retirement nest egg. Bart will definitely be working longer than he had otherwise thought and be living on less of his income than he had previously planned on.

This doesn't even begin to address the parenting issues. Bart and Jane could, of course, engage in positional bargaining, with Bart saying he wants the kids 50/50 and Jane responding that alternating weekends from Saturday morning to Sunday evening works just fine. Again, how is Jane going to react to Bart's 50/50 demand? I expect that small mushroom cloud you see in the distance is Jane's head blowing off her shoulders. That is matched by Bart's reaction to the restrictive proposal by Jane. Getting positional will deprive each person of the opportunity to talk (and be *heard*) about what concerns them—like Jane's anxiety about seeing her role as primary caretaker for her children go through changes, or Bart's worry about losing contact with his children. After all, it *is* terribly painful to switch from a life in which your children are always living under your roof to one in which you have them with you part of the time (whatever that part might be).

These are the kinds of things that appear on the collaborative lawyer's radar. I sometimes wonder if the best collaborative lawyers I've come across are therapists with briefcases. These people develop a real sensitivity to the dynamics of divorce and everybody's struggle with huge life changes.

Conventional lawyers are quick to point out the great risks attendant to collaborative practice. The most obvious of these arises from the withdrawal provision in the Participation Agreement (if anyone goes to court, then each lawyer has to withdraw, and new litigation counsel has to be retained). For sure, the hardship of hiring a lawyer, telling them your story, building a relationship with them, and paying them a lot of money, only to have to do it all over again with someone else if the case "falls out" of the collaborative process, is huge. Most people simply don't have the money to start all over again with a new lawyer, so they are stuck. While this is an important consideration, it's not a reason to reject collaborative practice. It *is* a reason to vet the heck out of the people you are going to use. A successful collaborative case will have experienced (or at least very committed) *collaborative* lawyers and other professionals involved. After all, this approach is not only for people who get along just fine, flinging daisies of peace and love left and right. There are often serious conflicts which involve infidelity, financial waste, drug/alcohol use, or escalating anger between partners. Bottom line: If you believe your divorce might be difficult because there are a number of things at the outset that you and your spouse feel strongly about *and* disagree about, make sure you have professionals who have thought carefully about operating within the collaborative framework.

Collaborative lawyers are committed to supporting their clients in making decisions that are right for them—decisions that take in both *legal* and *non-legal* factors. Unlike conventional lawyers, who speak for their clients, collaborative lawyers (and the other professionals on the collaborative divorce team) encourage people to have their own voice. After all, one abiding truth in all of this is that a time will come when all these professionals will be part of your past and you will be left with the other parent of your kids—someone with whom you will need to communicate, coordinate, and *exist* for many years to come. It is commonly said that you want to be able to dance with your ex-spouse at your children's weddings. One collaborative coach in the Northwest tells clients that his hope for them, in their post-divorce relationship, is that on a day, far in the future, when one of them passes, their children will be able to share that loss with the surviving parent, and they will be held and loved throughout that process—without the interference of bitterness, resentment, and vestiges of a hardened heart.

"Well, that's all well and good," you might say, "but seriously how realistic is it *honestly* to pull off what you're talking about?" The collaborative process is actually quite successful. Research conducted by the IACP reveals that about the same percentage of collaborative cases settle as conventional cases. This figure is in the high 90th percentile. Paradoxically, this is a basis thrown up by conventional divorce litigators for why people should *not* pursue collaborative divorce. "After all," they say, "if the odds of settling are the same, why take the risk of having to switch to a whole new set of lawyers if the case doesn't settle?" This critique entirely misses the point. The *quality* of the settlement reached through a collaborative process is much higher than the settlement that is generally squeezed out of alienated people in an all-day sweat session for the purposes of avoiding trial. Usually, the conventional settlement conference begins with the person running the show sitting both people and their lawyers down and reminding them of the thousands of dollars that will be spent if the case goes to trial *and* the uncertainty of outcome. The goal of settlement is not satisfaction and peace between parents, but avoidance of further (astronomical) expense. The settlement conference attempts to shove people out of their emotional mid-brains and into their logical cortical brains. The hope is that by the end of the day, there is enough logic-brain migration that good sense will prevail and a settlement will be reached. The drift back to emotion-brain can start the next day. It usually does. But the conventionally thinking lawyer believes she has done her job...and *she has*. It's just not the job that most of us need.

FOUNDATION:
THE PARTICIPATION AGREEMENT

So how is the laudable goal of a movement toward a mutually satisfactory settlement accomplished? The initial step is the acceptance of the terms of the first agreement that the people will sign. It is called the Participation Agreement, and it contains a number of unique and important terms. In fact, the elements that people are agreeing to are so important that the lawyers and clients spend the first half-hour of the first meeting reading the Participation Agreement aloud. I always think of the Passover *Seder* when experiencing this process, as each person goes around the table reading aloud a section of the agreement. Not all professionals choose to go through this read-through, opting, rather, to summarize the sections. A copy of a Participation Agreement currently utilized by some lawyers in the Pacific Northwest is in the Appendix. (Note that U.C.L.A. referenced there is not the university in California.[25])

Now let's stop for a moment and consider the obvious objections. Paying two lawyers to sit and read something out loud with us seems like a ridiculous waste of time and money. "I know how to read, for goodness sake. Let me take this home and read it, sign it, and start taking care of the business we're paying for from the start." While this objection certainly makes sense, there are two important reasons to go through this seemingly unnecessary exercise. First, people need to understand that they are passing through an entryway to a different, and not necessarily intuitive, dispute resolution process. The reading aloud of the Participation Agreement has a ritualistic quality that helps people understand that their collaborative process is beginning. A second reason is that reading the agreement aloud permits any questions to be aired and satisfactorily answered. If the lawyer just gives the agreement to the client and invites him to call with any questions, odds are that the client will read it and say he doesn't have any questions. Yet, experience shows that just about *every time* people walk carefully through the agreement, questions arise. Additionally, what they are committing to is both powerful and counter-intuitive to some people:

Good Faith: Take a moment and think about what this term means to you. It is far from what is expected in the old-fashioned divorce. In fact, traditional lawyers think it is folly to expect people in an adversarial relationship to voluntarily act in good faith. Actually, it's folly *not* to expect this, since divorcing people will be dealing with one another on their own in fairly short order. Here are the elements of good faith as described in the Participation Agreement used in the Northwest:

- Acting with honesty, transparency, and candor; Demonstrating cooperation, respect, integrity, and dignity
- Identifying and addressing the interests and needs of all
- Focusing on the future well-being of ourselves and our children
- Committing to resolve matters directly and without court intervention

If you want to end up with a high-level agreement, why hide information or be dishonest? If you are seeking to have a relationship with your former partner that will allow you to get on with your task of recovery and positive redirection of your life, why would you not seek to cooperate and respect the other? Since a divorce impacts a number of important people in your future, why would you not search for solutions that benefit the other person and your children?

The basic declaration of good faith and commitment to its tenets forms an essential foundation for future interaction. Happily, there is a team of professionals who can guide you as you work through what this might mean in your specific situation.

Focusing on the Future*:* Divorcing people naturally look to the past. Whether it's to find meaning for what has happened or to protect oneself against expected violation, looking back is the most common direction for those managing a divorce transition. It takes a bit of effort to wrench our gaze toward the future, but that is what we've got to do. As paradoxical as this seems, we need to stop discounting our partner's ability to perform in the future based upon disappointments of the past. Of all the expectations for divorcing people, this is usually the hardest to fathom. Yet, it is essential. You are not going to get positive, productive conduct from another if you are letting them know you expect the worst from them. One of the bad habits adopted during a failed relationship is the blindness (and lack of acknowledgment) for positive behavior, usually punctuated with quick comment about disappointments. With a little help, people can shift their thinking, slowly, yet effectively, over time. (Of course, there are plenty of people who will disappoint, being constitutionally incapable of acting out of anything but *self*-interest. For those people who seem to lack the capacity for empathy, the clear boundaries of legal agreements or court orders will be needed. These might not be attainable through consent and will require court intervention. For these people, collaborative divorce will be inappropriate. Yet, past disappointments are *not* proof of an absence of empathy, and often a professional who is not emotionally invested, the way a spouse is, can help illuminate this fact.)

Reinforcing that this is a Settlement Process: While all attorneys will say they are experts in settlement, collaborative lawyers, and the financial and mental health professionals who assist them, have a special obligation. The option of going to court has been voluntarily eliminated. Unlike lawyers in conventional divorce, where, if the clients don't agree, counsel have the option of saying, "Okay, then, I respect that we disagree; let's have a judge decide this," failure to settle in a collaborative divorce is a huge burden. So we change our head-space. If there is conflict, that's okay. It doesn't mean you can't work it out. It just means that you have to take a deep breath and return to the discussion. All the professionals have spent a lot of their own money and time in order to train in this particular area of dispute resolution. (In fact, lawyers almost always will make less money in a collaborative case than in a litigated case.) These people have made a strong personal and professional commitment to help people arrive at a durable settlement.

Complete Disclosure and Interest-Based Negotiation: A few years ago I met with a couple interested in pursuing a collaborative divorce process and wanting some basic information. He was an executive with a local Fortune 500 business and a professional negotiator. He was quite interested in collaborative law until I made it clear that complete transparency—sharing of all relevant information—was necessary. I saw his eyes glaze over and, after another twenty minutes of nodding and letting his wife ask questions, he left with her, never to return. Information is king in conventional, positional bargaining. A huge part of any negotiation process involves investigation of the position of the other side and asking questions to understand their strengths and weaknesses, their needs and concerns. He with the greater information about the other has power in negotiations. If you understand the other person's interests, but withhold your own, you have *power* because you can leverage their needs and interests to get more of what you want (while they can't do that to you). In agreeing to complete transparency, you give up that leverage—but you gain so much more in the end. Now you can both work to an outcome that will have the greatest probability of satisfying both people.

The key to this process is converting "positions" to "interests." The father who insists on "50/50 parenting" needs to be encouraged to talk about his need for meaningful contact and parenting authority with his children and how that can be accomplished. The wife who digs her heels in at $2,000 per month in alimony needs to be encouraged to talk about her budget and plans for the future. Usually after a marriage of fifteen years or more, with a substantial portion of that time seeing the mom out of the workforce, there has to be a discussion about what her plans are. He will have an obligation to assist her as she transitions into being self-supporting, and she will have an obligation to think this through and be reasonable and realistic about her expectations (just ask Mel, the previous chapter's mediator). For every position staked out by a disputant, there is almost always a decent, and relatable, set of personal interests being impacted.

There are many meaningful discussions that divorcing spouses have in the collaborative law context that they would either *never* consider in conventional divorce or which would lead them to a huge fight in court. The guy who's been working a job he hates and has truly wanted for years to make a transition, now being faced with having to support his ex and their kids; the mom who is using a lot of Xanax to get through the divorce but adamantly denies that she has a drug dependency; the dad who can't let go of the fact that his wife has left him for another woman and doesn't understand how this has absolutely no relevance to the divorce terms; the mom who has been in the area for only two years (this is where Dad grew up) and who now wants to move with her three- and five-year-old daughters to the other end of the country where her close and supportive family lives—these are but a handful of the struggles people bring with them into their divorce and which a court can't or won't adequately resolve. They'll get their court order, but that doesn't mean the issue will feel *resolved*. All *can* be addressed to the satisfaction of each participant in the collaborative process.

THE FOUNDATION:
HIGH-END GOALS

Sometimes I think of clients in the collaborative process as wriggling puppies in our grasp. There is so much history, repetitive behavior, and emotional triggering that, as much as one tries to pick them up and hold them, they will try to get free and...well, do what they do. The Participation Agreement is one way of saying, "Shhhh, it's okay" to these uncomfortable people who constantly want to wrest free and do what they've been doing for years. As with all anxious people, if divorcing partners know what to expect, that will go a long way toward settling them down and easing their misgivings about the unseen monster waiting around the corner. The next calming move is the discussion of what we in the Northwest call the couple's "High-End Goals." Other collaborative communities call this a Mission Statement. These describe the outcome each person would like to see when the divorce process is over. What do they want for themselves, their children, and each other in the future? This isn't a time to talk about specific goals, like, "I want the house," or, "I want to continue to put $1,000 per month into my retirement." The goals are much broader and might be another way of answering the question, "Why are you choosing this process?" (Hint: "To stay out of court" is *far* from the whole answer.) The kinds of responses that are the most common, because they reflect such universal concerns of divorcing people, run along these lines:

- To make sure our children are taken care of
- To support our children's relationships with each of us
- Financial security
- A chance to pursue a career
- To still have a relationship with my in-laws
- To be able to dance at our children's weddings (People *do* say that)

These goals are written down on large sheets of paper and, at the end of the meeting, those sheets are folded or rolled up and held onto by one of the lawyers, ready for retrieval and reminder when waters get choppy.

Many is the time that a spouse will get cranky in the middle of the process and want to smack the other. The heart rate jumps, the outrage surges, the old injuries pipe up for recognition. During these periods of distress and impending polarization, reminding either or both of their High-End Goals will recalibrate their senses. This is one of the greatest tools available to the collaborative professional. It's not unlike the weekly visit to church, as a process to remind people of their better selves—of what they aspire to be.

COLLABORATIVE LAW IS PART OF A BROAD REVOLUTIONARY SHIFT

Can you imagine a legal system in which lawyers seek to encourage greater empathy and compassion between their clients and their supposed adversaries...and in which the objective of a legal proceeding is to heal through greater understanding rather than crushing one's opponent and maximizing one's own self-interest? (In six months) lawyers, law professors and law students from around the country will gather in New York with exactly this aim—to envision and design a new legal system that seeks to fundamentally challenge the idea that lawyers should conduct themselves as if they are adversarial gladiators out to win legal battles at any cost and instead discuss how law and justice can be a vehicle for building understanding and community. This is the message attached to the brochure of the conference sponsored by The Project for Integrating Spirituality, Law and Politics.

Just as the Collaborative Law movement was sparking the imagination of thousands of divorce professionals, other new and "healing" approaches to law and legal education have taken hold. In the world of legal education, Professor Lawrence Krieger at Florida State College of Law wrote a groundbreaking article about law students' well-being. His work prompted the rise of a group of professors seeking to "humanize legal education." Annual conferences on the topic have drawn ever larger numbers of enthusiastic participants, who are teaching courses emphasizing counseling and social intelligence in the practice.

Years before this, law professors David Wexler and Bruce Winick developed the approach they called *Therapeutic Jurisprudence*, stating that the practice of law can be psychologically harmful for all participants. Their goal was to find procedures that would soften the damage caused by the aggression so often found in the law. Like Collaborative Law, TJ recognizes that truly satisfying results come from an interdisciplinary approach—here, the meshing of law and psychology.

Restorative Justice has been a part of the criminal justice system for many years now. Used mostly with juvenile offenders, it fosters dialogue between perpetrators and victims of crime—seeking to promote recognition of harm done and remorse in one, and healing and forgiveness in the other. YouTube is full of moving examples of this most powerful social justice tool at work.

Transformative Mediation was created by law professor Robert A. Baruch Bush and communications professor Joseph Folger. They were pushing back against the prevailing belief in the mediation field that a "fair settlement" (usually judged by the "objective" standards of the mediator) defined the optimal outcome in mediation. Folger and Bush described a different set of values to be embraced in mediation. The most important were *Empowerment*, in which the participants created their own solution, which worked for *them*, outside of the opinions of non-involved third parties about that "objective" best solution; and *Recognition*, which describes the ability to empathize with the other person (or group) and express that empathy. Folger and Bush were among the first to state the simple notion that in true conflict resolution, each person must be able to stand in the shoes of the other.

These are just a few examples of a movement that has been sweeping the legal world over the past twenty years, which many within it refer to as *Law as a Healing Profession*. Many thousands of practitioners, together with allied professionals from the mental health, financial, law enforcement, teaching, and other fields have embraced this philosophy. You won't find references to them in the television dramas or news programs, which emphasize conflict and battle (because these are sexy and sell). However, this Comprehensive Law

Movement (so-named by law professor and commentator Susan Daicoff) will reward any web search with hundreds of valuable and heartening links. As with almost any worrying trend in our modern time, there is a parallel, and healing, alternative, if we only seek it out.

Adam and Beth and Helen and William and Lani

The five-way collaborative meeting was only five minutes old when Beth, tearful and clearly shaken, nodded when Helen asked her client if she needed a break. Lani, the coach, asked if she could go with them, and both assented. The three left to go to Helen's office down the hall, leaving William and Adam alone in the conference room, munching on the nuts and fruit in the bowls before them. "Well, we had to cross this bridge eventually," William said, patting his client on the shoulder.

"I know, I know—but I really didn't think it would be such a big deal. She's known about Susie since we split up. I wish she'd calm down. I never even kissed her before I moved out and Beth and I were through," said Adam as he popped a cashew into his mouth. William went to the bathroom while Adam scrolled through the email on his phone. It took fifteen minutes for the others to return.

The three women had gone to Helen's office without a word and, immediately upon sitting down, Beth gripped her tissue and pounded her knee. "I am so sorry," she said, the emotion still leaking through her vocal cords. "I thought I was ready to have this conversation, but when he just sits there and says he's moving in with Susie like it's the most natural thing in the world, I want to strangle him. What *right* does he have to subject our children to his drama?" Helen and Lani gave the briefest of glances at one another, providing assurance they were on the same page.

The professional team had spoken about the meeting the day before in a one-hour conference call. Jeff, the financial specialist, and Nora, the child specialist, had been on the call, despite the fact that they weren't going to be attending the meeting the next day. If the team was going to support these people, they would need to be cohesive, with everybody in the loop. These conference calls were not frequent, with maybe two or three during the entire course of any one case, but Adam and Beth's divorce was moving toward a critical juncture and everybody's involvement was going to be important. Nora had spoken with Jason and Lilly at some length and had sent around a "Professional Team Only" email, which candidly described her observations. Both young people knew what was going on with Susie and their dad, Nora had related. They both loved their father—in fact, they both *liked* their father as well—but each had shared with Nora that he acted more like a kid sometimes than an adult. They both thought Susie was "nice," but were also upset at both their dad and Susie, because their mother was so sad all the time because of them. Lilly, particularly, didn't want to be around their dad and Susie right now, while Jason didn't seem to care one way or the other. He just wanted to make sure his dad was going to have an Xbox at his place.

Most of the telephone conference the day before had pivoted around William's disclosure that Adam was going to move in with Susie in a month but had not yet informed Beth or the kids. The team had talked about how to handle this potentially explosive disclosure and agreed that it had to be addressed in some way at the next day's meeting. To make believe that Adam hadn't told William, particularly since the whole purpose of the next day's meeting was to work through a residential schedule for the kids, would have been impossible. They'd spend a couple of hours getting a plan together, and then it would blow up when Adam told Beth, and Beth understood that this was information that Adam and everyone else had withheld from her in the five-way. The damage control would have been unnecessarily expensive and probably fruitless to boot. Helen, William, and Lani had met for a half-hour pre-brief prior to the clients showing up (as was the norm) and had talked about the agenda for the day. It was their practice to create an agenda so the clients could start a meeting with some guidance and a foundation for the discussions to come, with a request to the clients to supplement what had been written on the large Post-it sheet on the wall. The sheet awaiting Adam and Beth had said:

- Check-in
- Report from Adam and Beth on how current residential schedule is working
- On line co-parenting calendar options
- Discussion of Nora's report to parents on kids' status

- Kids' exposure to Susie
- Jason and homework/computer game discussion
- Craft residential schedule

When the meeting had begun, and after Lani had read the agenda and asked if there was anything either wanted to add, Adam had said that he was planning to move in with Susie in a month, and that needed to be discussed. That's when Beth had to exit, and the three women adjourned to Helen's office.

Helen and Lani now looked back at Beth, who continued, dabbing at her eyes with a tissue, "Goddammit, why is he so fucking selfish?" Tears started streaming down her cheeks again. "I'm sorry. I hate to cry!"

"Don't worry about it," Helen assured her. "Take whatever time you need to steady yourself, and let's talk this through."

Beth gave a tight-lipped, tearful smile, took a deep breath, and let it out slowly. "Thank you. I feel better." She got up to throw away her tissue and, still standing, looked down on the other women and said, "Here's the thing. I know it's ridiculous for me to be upset over Adam and Susie since I'm the one who wanted the divorce—"

"Not so fast," Lani said, her hand raised in a "stop" gesture. "I have known people who were remarried and still had a strong emotional reaction when their ex-spouse partnered up. It's all very new for you and, even if you chose to end this marriage, it doesn't mean that you automatically stop thinking of yourself as coupled with Adam. That takes time and healing."

Helen added, "It would be great if both people could recouple at exactly the same time after an agreed-upon appropriate healing period, but you know, that never happens."

Beth sat back down, nodding. "I know, and I appreciate the insight. I'll be fine. I know that. But it's the kids who are going to suffer through this." Tears again brimmed in Beth's eyes.

"You really want to make sure you protect your brood, don't you?" smiled Lani.

"You bet your ass!" was the immediate reply, as Beth straightened her back and looked straight into each woman's eyes. "It makes me so angry that he can just go off and do what he damn well pleases. He's always been that way. Now he wants to shove that little slut in my babies' faces and I'm not going to let him. I refuse, and if he doesn't like it, he can take me to court!"

"Okay, Beth," Helen said softly, leaning forward and touching her knee, "Take a deep breath…again. This is something we definitely need to talk about before we go back in there." Helen glanced at her notes and then continued, "First, remember how Nora said both Lilly and Jason are doing fine. Lilly's angry at her father, and she isn't shy. She has already told him that she doesn't want to be there when Susie is around. I think the conversation we need to have with Adam is how he puts together Lilly's statement and deciding to live with Susie. That's something I think we need to do today." Beth visibly relaxed and eased against the back cushion of the chair. "Jason seems fine with anything right now and appears to have taken this whole Susie thing in stride. Is there anything that you have seen that would make you think otherwise?"

Beth shook her head. "Not really. That boy is either a little Buddha or completely oblivious. Either way," she smiled at the thought, "he does seem to be doing okay."

"One more thing to think about before we go back in there," added Lani. "Remember when you and Adam and the lawyers had your first meeting where you read the Participation Agreement?"

Beth nodded, "Yes, I remember that."

"Well," continued Lani, "you both also talked about what you wanted out of this process— we called it your 'high-end goals.' I'm sure you remember that." Again, a nod from Beth. "Helen, do you have your notes of what those high-end goals were for Adam and Beth?"

"Yes, I do," replied Helen, as she paged backward through her file. "Beth, both you and Adam separately said that your highest goal was for the children to come out of this process secure and cared for, and that each of you would do what you could to support them through the divorce. Another goal you each shared was that you wanted to come out of this process with a solid co-parental relationship. It seems to me that we ought to return to these goals when we go back in there, so that our discussions will have that as a context. What do you think?"

"I definitely agree," said Beth. "I'd like to see how he talks his way out of that."

"Well, you might be surprised," replied Helen. "In our conference call yesterday, William told us that Adam isn't finding this as easy as you might think. He says that he and Susie are getting serious, and it doesn't make sense for them to live separately. At the same time, he knows this is complicated for the kids—particularly for Lilly—and he wants to do what's best for her. He has said that the 50/50 shared parenting idea isn't realistic, and he understands that. He wants to work something out so that, for a while at least, Susie won't be around when the kids come over."

"Well, I have to tell you I'm skeptical about that. Adam is extremely charming and tells people what he thinks they want to hear. What if Lilly still doesn't want to come over? Can he force her?" Beth asked, her forehead crinkled quizzically.

"That's what we are here to talk about today, among other things," replied Helen, her hand again squeezing Beth's knee. "We can't promise that you and Adam will come to any agreements. All we can promise is that we will work as hard as we can to create a space where you can be heard, and we will also try to help you understand Adam's perspective in a way so that you don't want to send him down the elevator shaft." Beth laughed at that image and said, "Thanks. I feel better. Let's go in and get this thing done." Helen and Lani were both relieved for the moment that the crisis they had feared just might be averted.

"WHAT WOULD THE JUDGE DO?"

It might seem unimaginable that someone would go through a divorce process using lawyers and not want to know *what the judge would do.* Yet, collaborative lawyers will rarely talk about this. It would be easy and quite natural for Helen to say reassuringly to Beth that if this went to court, the judge would not force a child to reside with their father and his new girlfriend so soon after separation. *Certainly* no judge would order a 50/50 residential arrangement, like Adam has been pressing for, under these circumstances. Yet, Helen doesn't say these things to her client. Why is that?

Different professionals may give different answers to this question. Here's mine: The court system is, essentially, a coercive process. As we saw earlier, any decision by a judge comes after each side has dug in and argued why their side should prevail. To reference what a judge would do is to inject the element of coercion into a voluntary and cooperative process. That's different from discussing the law and general legal principles. A state's laws concerning divorce (property division, caring for children, providing support) reflect one important (but not exclusive) set of standards for how things ought to be done. Discussing the standards set by a state's laws is, I believe, different from talking about what the judge would do.

So often, people who are sick to death of trying, on their own, to deal with the disappointments and frustrations of interacting with their spouse, just want someone to *make* that person do what they should. When they learn that this won't happen in a collaborative divorce process, they often express disappointment. Well...they express disappointment until they begin to understand how much *making* them do something will cost, if they went to court. What if they could, with the help of professionals, get the other to voluntarily cooperate? Honest to God, that is what happens in collaborative cases. It defies personal history, intuition, and years' worth of negative expectations. It's possible, because this is what collaborative divorce professionals *do for a living*. It's what they're good at. Conflict doesn't render them frightened or dispirited. So, there is no need to resort to, "What would a court do?" thinking. You can work it out. Have faith. You're not alone in this.

Adam and Beth and Helen and William and Lani, Redux

After Adam had been through his email and William had returned from nature's call, the lawyer asked his client, "How're you doing?"

"Okay...but that was pretty intense," Adam replied while nervously crunching on a Brazil nut. "I must be nervous," he thought to himself, "eating one of these things. I hate Brazil nuts!"

"Is it okay to quickly go through what we talked about yesterday?" asked William.

William had been a collaborative lawyer for a dozen years and knew his way around the process. One thing he had picked up from Holly, one of the earliest and best practitioners in the community, was that he never went into a four-way or five-way meeting without having sat with his client the day or so before and made sure they were prepared. One of his greatest aggravations in practice was walking into meetings with a client's spouse who was clearly unprepared. He enjoyed working with Helen for precisely that reason. She had the temperament and work ethic to make a collaborative case run as smoothly as it could. Sometimes that wasn't so smooth, but he never looked at Helen as anything but a facilitative presence in these cases.

In fact, when Adam had first come to him, saying that his wife was divorcing him, William had recommended that she call Helen. As with everything William did as an attorney, he was thoughtfully and impeccably professional. His first meetings with clients were a uniform ninety minutes, a good portion of which was spent describing the different process options. While he did not want clients to automatically turn to conventional divorce litigation without considering mediation and collaborative law, he certainly was open to their taking the more-travelled road. If that was the choice, he referred the client to a handful of colleagues in the community who were decent people and very solid lawyers. He didn't litigate any more.

That had been an important transition for him, taken some five years before. William came to realize he could not do both conventional litigation and collaborative law. The mind-sets were so conflicting that if he worked a collaborative case right after an intense, adversarial settlement conference, he was too aggressive and pissed people off. If he worked a litigated case after a few collaborative meetings, he found the other lawyer to be annoyingly aggressive, and then he got pissed off. He didn't do his best work either way, so he jettisoned litigation. That had meant a drop-off in income. He had talked to his husband, and they had agreed that they could budget around it. William cut his overhead. His longtime paralegal had much less to do if William wasn't litigating, so he made sure that she got enough part-time work with colleagues and cut her time by three-quarters. It had been the smartest thing he ever did, work-wise.

He remembered in their first meeting that Adam had been really angry at Beth. At the same time, though, he had this "live and let live" attitude and preferred not to get mired in some drawn out and expensive legal fight. William had given Adam Shaub's book on divorce (he always had a few in his office to give to potential clients) and, a couple days later, Adam had called to retain his services. The next thing that happened was odd by conventional practice standards.

William had recommended that Beth call Helen. He remembers Adam's immediate response, "Why would Beth call a lawyer that *my* lawyer recommended?"

"Good question," William responded. "Collaborative cases aren't easy. The lawyers have to get along and trust each other. Helen is an excellent practitioner and I think Beth will like her. I have successfully worked with Helen in the past. Believe me, you want a good attorney representing your wife. It will save time and money and increase the chances of successfully completing this process by a huge factor."

Since Beth hadn't wanted a legal battle, she was open to considering a collaborative divorce and, after vetting Helen and then meeting her, she had retained Helen as her lawyer. Now they were into their third, and most important, meeting. "This," thought William, as he waited for the return of the three women to the conference room, "is where the rubber meets the road in this case." Each divorce has its own hot-button issues, and Adam's relationship with Susie was one of the two big ones in this one. (The other was getting Beth the help she needed to become decently self-supporting.)

"Man, I just wish she hadn't done that," said Adam. "It's always some drama with Beth."

"Well, we talked about that, right?" replied William. "Are you still okay talking to her about this?"

"I guess. Bring it on. We've got to do it some time," said Adam as he leaned forward in his chair, elbows on the table, staring at the agenda on the wall as the women reentered the room.

"I'm sorry," said Beth as she sat down. "I just needed to catch my breath. Where were we?"

"I'm sorry too, Beth," Adam said, looking directly at her. "I know that felt like I dropped a bomb in here, and I do apologize for that. I just didn't know how to talk to you about my living situation, and I believed this would be the best and safest place to figure this out." Adam picked up the water glass. He was nervous and his mouth was dry. The pause helped calm his nerves. "I want to do the best thing for Lilly and Jason, but this relationship with Susie is important to me and, to be honest, I don't like living alone. Her lease and mine are up within a month of each other's and it just made sense to do this. I mean, Beth, you left me."

"Wait a minute—" Beth interrupted.

Before this exchange could go further, Lani cut in, "Okay, Beth, Adam, slow down, here. This is a tough subject for you. Let's keep our eyes on the prize. How are you going to work together to solve this problem?" The attention in the room was on the coach as she smiled and continued.

"Adam, you have been clear from the beginning that you want...you feel you need to pursue this relationship. You're a smart guy. You understand that there are risks to getting involved so quickly after you separate. You and I talked about this in our individual meeting, and I know William has talked to you about that. Obviously this is very important to you."

Turning to Beth, who had been seated next to Adam for the meeting, Lani continued, "We've also talked about how hard this is for you, Beth, but if this is something Adam feels he needs to do for himself, you're not going to stop him...at least in this process. So we need to figure out how to make this work for you. I have heard you say that the two hardest things about Adam's relationship with Susie is that it's hard for you to digest, for obvious reasons, and also that you want to protect your children from confusion and upset. Do I have that right?"

After Beth nodded confirmation, Lani turned again to Adam and asked him a question she knew he was ready to answer, based on the team conference the day before. "So, Adam...you have given this a lot of thought, I'm sure. What ideas do you have as far as the children are concerned?"

Given this cue, Adam started, "Beth, I have done a lot of thinking about this. I know it feels too soon for me to be with someone else, but I never planned this. I don't want to hurt you or Lilly and Jason. I want to be able to get on with my life and heal. I think Susie can help me do that." Again, Adam paused to take a drink.

"I think the kids would really like Susie and she definitely does not want to take your place as their mother. There is not a chance in hell she could ever do that. You are their mom, and I feel so lucky that you are the mother of my children. I could not imagine a better person."

He looked at Beth to emphasize his sincerity (it had been hard to look directly at her except for a few bits, because he had felt so nervous). He saw that her eyes had moistened as she looked at him.

"The kids belong with you as their primary home. It makes no sense to force them to live half the time with me and Susie. I know that a court wouldn't go there and you know what? I can understand that. But I want to be with them, so here is what I am thinking. For the next few months—and we can talk about how long that will be—Susie has agreed to spend long weekends with her friends Bill and Melinda. They have a spare room and have known her for a long time. I'd like Jason and Lilly to stay with me Thursday nights to Monday mornings every other weekend. Susie won't be around. For the first few months, I'll see that there are no pictures or other obvious signs of her around the house. We'll talk over the next few months about how we integrate our kids more into my life with Susie. If Lilly doesn't want to come over because she's mad at me, I want to follow up on Lani's suggestion and see a counselor with our daughter to work this out. If it takes some time, then so be it, but I don't want my relationship with them to be any more damaged than it might already have been."

Adam could see Beth easing back into her chair, looking directly at him. "I trust you, Beth. I don't know why you decided to divorce me. Maybe I'll figure it out some day, but it doesn't hurt the way it did.... Anyway, that's not important right now. Jason and Lilly are what's important. I'd like to also work with you to arrange one-on-one time with each of them. Maybe dinners every couple of weeks, or Jason can come over for a weekend if Lilly isn't ready yet. It'll still just be me and him but no Susie. I'll make sure I get an Xbox for him." Adam smiled and was surprised and pleased to see Beth smiling as well. "So, what do you say? Can we figure this out together?"

Had Adam not received counsel from both Lani and William, he likely could never have figured out what to say or how to say it. But this statement by him was a breakthrough moment for them. Beth still had misgivings about Adam's judgment and Susie's presence, but she understood some of that to be natural and based on her history with Adam and the whiplash rapidity of his coupling with Susie. She had always known Adam to be a basically sincere person and believed he was truly making an honest effort. She smiled and said, "I can work with that."

They got through the day's agenda fairly easily after that, and, after one more meeting to work through the financial issues in the divorce, Adam and Beth could truly say that they had experienced a "successful" divorce.

WHY COLLABORATIVE PRACTICE WORKS

While sceptics and "realists" might dismiss this scenario as cooked up and unbelievable, I can assure you that this exchange and its like are repeated daily in all corners of the country (and beyond). Take a look at the Appendix and you will see that almost every state has a robust collaborative law community.

There are two factors that make outcomes like Beth and Adam's resolution about Susie and the kids possible. First is the complete commitment by every member of the team to this process. Each person (attorney, mental health professional, and financial specialist) embarks on a course of extensive and expensive training. They add vital skills to the conventional strengths they already possessed. The second factor accompanies all success in any endeavor: Preparation. The team in Adam and Beth's divorce *talked to each other* about goals and approach. Helen was able to stand beside Beth and make her need for care and attention to the children's needs clear. William was able to present Adam as not some irresponsible, child-harming doofus, but as a man struggling with his post-divorce transition and a person of essential goodwill. Disagree with his choices, but these don't make him a bad person who is to be shunned or shamed.

As with any *system*, there will often arise a tendency to marginalize a particularly difficult or unreasonable player. Professionals must guard against the tendency of one of the lawyers, the coach, and financial professional to see one of the spouses as incorrigible, overly difficult, crazy, mean-spirited, or in some other way an impediment to the process. Sometimes the klieg light will shine on one of the lawyers, who has not been able to set down his adversarial thinking and will aggressively advocate for his client in a way that shoves everybody else into corners. If this dynamic is allowed to proceed unchecked, then somebody is going to be scapegoated. When somebody is scapegoated, it is *they* who feel cornered and excluded, and you can bet the farm that they will become more defensive and aggressive. How do you think *that's* going to turn out?

I want to make one final comment about, and tip my imaginary hat to, those lawyers who chose to engage in this often challenging collaborative approach. When you represent a client in a conventional lawsuit, there are no ambiguities. You go for whatever you can reasonably obtain, and there is no compunction about painting the other spouse in the darkest colors available to you. This time-worn approach to divorce litigation will likely guarantee the unfailing trust of your client. The collaborative lawyer's task, however, is more complicated. You must work to understand the needs and humanity of your client's spouse. You might even find yourself speaking empathically to that person in the presence of your client in an effort to understand what is driving them. There will be times when you clearly articulate the other person's needs in front of your client. "Whose lawyer *are* you?" is the question that inexperienced collaborative lawyers fear the most. The solution to this is quite simple, and it has been mastered by every committed collaborative lawyer who represents a client.

In order to succeed in this arena, you must take the time and make the effort to *hear your own client*. Find out what drives them. Learn what they fear. Determine what support they need (therapeutic? social? vocational?) and see that they receive it. The high-level collaborative lawyer's first and greatest task is to assure your client that you "get" them, you support them, you accept them…that you truly care about what happens to them. Once you have achieved that, your client's anxiety about your allegiances will diminish to wisps of smoke and float away. Lawyers never guarantee anything…but that's about as close to a guarantee as I can give.

TAKEAWAYS

- **Collaborative divorce can be managed by most people— but not everyone. Each person must engage in an honest personal inventory of their motivations and capacity to pursue a collaborative process. Some of the questions you need to ask yourself are in the Appendix.**

- The collaborative divorce process is about much more than just staying out of court or saving money.
- Review the model Participation Agreement that is in the Appendix. Determine for yourself if you can engage in a process bounded by the rules and principles of this agreement.
- Before you meet with a lawyer, write down two sets of questions. One should involve your substantive concerns. The other should contain your process questions. (Examples of these include: How long will the process take? Have you worked with the other lawyer before? What is your impression of him or her? What do I need to do to make this process run more smoothly?)

FINAL THOUGHTS

Conventional litigation attorneys frequently express grave misgivings about Collaborative Law, noting that the process leaves a vulnerable partner wide open for exploitation. When people rely on trust and good faith in resolving disputes, the person who trusts and exercises that good faith will surely be at the mercy of the person who does not. People *cannot* enter a collaborative process for the primary purpose of staying out of court. If that is the major driver, you will not recognize the hard work that is entailed in successfully negotiating through a collaborative law process. To repeat the words which began this book, divorce will rock you to your core, whether you struggle with the long process of disengagement and are the "leaver" or if you are suddenly faced with an unexpected life change and are the "left." You have to think very carefully about how you wish to proceed. Mediation and collaborative practice can save many couples from the avoidable trauma of conventional divorce. Frequently over the years, I have looked at a couple at the end of mediation or collaborative divorce and known with certainty that their chosen process saved them from expense and heartache. At the same time, I have worked with some couples for whom these approaches have failed, usually because of the failure of the professionals to identify the factors of coercion or withholding of information that rendered the process exploitive, rather than healing.

In reviewing these pages one final time before sending them off in final form, I see that I am an optimist at heart. I am inclined to give people the benefit of the doubt and view certain narrow, self-serving, and harmful behaviors as emanations of a fearful and uncertain heart, rather than venality and ill will. This is clearly not the book of a cynic. In saying this, I want to acknowledge the viewpoint of the cynics, who would say that the actions and outcomes I describe here are unrealistic, the product of a naïve attitude that might render us dangerously vulnerable to the malevolent or manipulative actor. I concede that this risk exists. Yet, I also ask, "What choice do we have, if we want to move toward outcomes that reflect our highest, best selves?" My most ardent hope is that you have found support and a bit more clarity within these pages. I wish you the very best on this transformative life journey.

A NOTE OF GRATITUDE

Where would I be without my dearest Beverly and our daughter, Dani, who is the light of my life? Up the creek without a paddle, that's where! Thank you for the years of love, joy, struggle, laugher, and *life*. The Mama, the Mama! The Daughter, the Daughter! Indeed. The villagers of Anatevka had it right.

To my brilliant chums who gave me exceptional feedback and guidance: Bev, Francine Gaillour, Tonia Sassi, Stevan Bosanac, Erin Marquardt, Victoria Livingston, Paul David, Stephen Faulstich, Mike Fancher, Don Desonier, Robert Ritchie, Neil Selman, Brad Lancaster and Steve Gaddis. Your contributions warmed my heart and filled my brain. Thank you Karen Bonnell for your constant encouragement.

To Jennifer D. Munro, who edited this manuscript with great care. Your work taught me more about writing than I could ever have imagined and I am eternally grateful for your kindness and intellect. Thanks for laughing at my jokes!

Thank you, Leonard Shaw, for your supportive words when I struggled with *whether* to do this. Your love is really quite boundless. Also to the other therapists and mentors who have touched me over the years: Jan Lustig, John McNeel, Peg Blackstone, Mary Blackburn, Ellen Ostrow, and Bill Cooper.

To my collaborative law colleagues who are so numerous and inspirational, and my EFT pals who are so full of compassion and intelligence.

And finally to my clients over the years, both legal and therapeutic. Allowing me to join with you in your journeys has always been, and remains, the greatest privilege of my life, which I will treasure always.

ENDNOTES

[1] My elevator speech is, "Hello! Do you know about collaborative divorce? No? Well let me…HEY, what was that loud metallic sound. Oh no! We're falling. Arrrghgh!"

[2] Bruce Fisher, in his wise and wonderful book, *Rebuilding: When Your Relationship Ends (1981)*, created one of the two clearest, shortest, most assuring books on the trauma and recovery from the end of an intimate relationship. The other is more about the process of transition, itself. It was written by William Bridges and bears the surprising title of *Transitions: Making Sense of Life's Changes* (2nd Ed.) (2004). Highly, highly recommended.

[3] Janet Johnston and Vivien Roseby, *In the Name of the Child: A Developmental Approach to Understanding and Helping Children of Conflicted and Violent Divorce (2009)*.

[4] Raoul Felder, *Divorce* (1971).

[5] Pauline Tesler, *Collaborative Law – Achieving Effective Resolution in Divorce without Litigation* (2001). Tesler is one of the original driving forces in the establishment and spread of the collaborative process in divorce. Her venerability is reflected in the fact that the American Bar Association's original guide in Collaborative Law was authored by Tesler. This book, cited above, is directed to lawyers and addresses all the questions and concerns legal professionals would raise about this process. Here, Tesler is quoting Judge Anne Kass's essay, *Clinical Advice from the Bench*. Two excellent books devoted solely to Collaborative Divorce and directed to the lay public are 2007's *Collaborative Divorce: A Revolutionary New Way to Restructure Your Family, Resolve Legal Issues and Move On*, by Pauline Tesler and therapist and early collaborative coach and trainer, Peggy Thompson, and *The Collaborative Way to Divorce: The Revolutionary New Method That Results in Less Stress, Lower Cost and Happier Kids – Without Going to Court*, by Collaborative Law's originator Stu Webb and one if its first active practitioners and trainers, Ron Ousky (a colleague of Webb's from Minneapolis), also published in 2007.

[6] Scalia's dissent was in the Supreme Court case *Jaffee vs. Redmond* (for the lawyers out there, the citation is 518 U.S. 1 [1996]). Mary Lu Redmond was a police officer in a suburb of Chicago when she was called out to an apartment disturbance. When she arrived, three women

ran out of the building, yelling that there had been a stabbing. Then two men burst out, one about to stab the other with a butcher knife. When they didn't stop, she shot and killed Ricky Allen. A nasty confrontation ensued with a crowd that gathered. Jaffee sued Redmond on behalf of Allen's estate. Some witnesses said that Redmond had her gun drawn before she left her cruiser and others said that there had been no knife. The whole incident was traumatic for Redmond, who left the force and entered therapy with a Licensed Clinical Social Worker. When lawyers wanted records of the fifty therapy sessions, Redmond's lawyers objected, saying they were "privileged" therapist/client communications. This case was in Federal Court, which has its own rules for how cases proceed, separate from the rules in each of the fifty states. The question was whether this privilege existed in Federal Court cases, preventing release of the therapist's records. Citing the laws in *every* state protecting these session notes from compulsory disclosure in a lawsuit, Justice John Paul Stevens wrote for the majority of the court in finding that the same privilege existed in Federal Courts, noting, "Treatment by a physician for physical ailments can often proceed successfully on the basis of a physical examination, objective information supplied by the patient, and the results of diagnostic tests. Effective psychotherapy, by contrast, depends upon an atmosphere of confidence and trust in which the patient is willing to make a frank and complete disclosure of facts, emotions, memories, and fears. Because of the sensitive nature of the problems for which individuals consult psychotherapists, disclosure of confidential communications made during counseling sessions may cause embarrassment or disgrace. For this reason, the mere possibility of disclosure may impede development of the confidential relationship necessary for successful treatment." Only Scalia and Justice Rehnquist disagreed with this reasoning.

[7] *Marriage of Iverson,* 11. Cal.App.4th 1497 (1992).

[8] Steven Keeva was a gem within the legal community. A long-time editor and writer with the ABA Journal, Keeva died prematurely from early onset Alzheimer's. He authored a wonderful article in the January, 1999 ABA Journal entitled: *Beyond Words: Understanding What Your Client is Really Saying Makes For Successful Lawyering.* It was a mainstay assignment during my dozen years of teaching Interviewing and Counseling to University of Washington law students. Keeva also wrote an influential book, *Transforming Practices* in 1999

(now in its 10th Edition), urging lawyers to pursue meaning in the work they do. He will be sorely missed.

[9] Abigail Trafford was a journalist who went through her own painful divorce, so she did what writers do. So, she interviewed scores of people—judges, lawyers, psychologists, divorced people—and then wrote about it. In a statement I have often quoted, Trafford describes divorce as a "savage emotional" experience. To be sure, this is not the case with many divorces, but the stresses exacted by the dissolution of this profound attachment relationship will always make descent into "crazy time" a real risk. The book helps explain the trough and helps people to extricate themselves from the pit. *Crazy Time* (1982) remains one of my most often recommended books for people going through the divorce process.

[10] Hetherington and John Kelly, *For Better or Worse: Divorce Reconsidered* (2002).

[11] Rhoda Feinberg and James Green, *The Intractable Client - Guidelines for Working With Personality Disorders in Family Law* (35 Family & Conciliation Courts Review 351 (1997).

[12] Bill Eddy, *High Conflict People in Legal Disputes, 4th Ed.* (2012). Bill Eddy was a therapist for many years before he went to law school and became a sought-after mediator, then sought-after speaker and trainer. Bill is currently the foremost expert on "high conflict" divorce and how people so afflicted can be supported through this highly destabilizing process. I strongly recommend that you visit Eddy's website, www.highconflictinstitute.com, for books, videos, and other valuable educational materials.

[13] Antisocial Personality Disorder
A pervasive pattern of disregard for and violation of the rights of others occurring since age of 15 years, as indicated by three (or more) of the following:

1. Failure to conform to social norms with respect to lawful behaviors as indicated by repeatedly performing acts that are grounds for arrest;
2. Deceitfulness, as indicated by repeated lying, use of aliases, or conning others for personal profit or pleasure;
3. Impulsivity or failure to plan ahead;
4. Irritability and aggressiveness, as indicated by repeated physical fights or assaults;
5. Reckless disregard for safety of self or others;

6. Consistent irresponsibility, as indicated by repeated failure to sustain consistent work behavior or honor financial obligations;
7. Lack of remorse, as indicated by being indifferent to or rationalizing having hurt, mistreated or stolen from another.

Borderline Personality Disorder
A pervasive pattern of instability of interpersonal relationships, self-image, and affects, and marked impulsivity beginning by early adulthood and present in a variety of contexts, as indicated by five (or more) of the following:
1. Frantic efforts to avoid real or imagined abandonment. **Note**: Do not include suicidal behavior or self-mutilating behavior covered in Criterion 5;
2. A pattern of unstable and intense interpersonal relationships characterized by alternating between extremes of idealization and devaluation;
3. Identity disturbance: markedly and persistently unstable self-image or sense of self;
4. Impulsivity in at least two areas that are potentially self-damaging (e.g., spending, sex, substance abuse, reckless driving, binge eating). **Note**: Do not include suicidal behavior or self-mutilating behavior covered in Criterion 5;
5. Recurrent suicidal behavior, gestures, threats, or self-mutilating behavior;
6. Affective instability due to a marked reactivity of mood (e.g., intense episodic dysphoria, irritability, or anxiety usually lasting a few hours and only rarely more than a few days);
7. Chronic feelings of emptiness;
8. Inappropriate intense anger or difficulty controlling anger (e.g., frequent displays of temper, constant anger, recurrent physical fights);
9. Transient, stress-related paranoid ideation or severe dissociative symptoms.

Narcissistic Personality Disorder
A pervasive pattern of grandiosity (in fantasy or behavior), need for admiration, and lack of empathy, beginning by early adulthood and present in a variety of contexts as indicated by five (or more) of the following:
1. Has grandiose sense of self-importance (exaggerates achievements and talents, expects to be recognized as superior without commensurate achievement);
2. Is preoccupied with fantasies or unlimited success, power,

brilliance, beauty or ideal love;
3. Believes that he or she is "special" and unique and can only be understood by, or should associate with, other special or high-status people (or institutions);
4. Requires excessive admiration;
5. Has a sense of entitlement (i.e., unreasonable expectations of especially favorable treatment or automatic compliance with his or her expectations);
6. Is interpersonally exploitive (i.e. takes advantage of others to achieve his or her own needs);
7. Lacks empathy: is unwilling to recognize or identify with the feelings and needs of others;
8. Is envious of others or believes that others are envious of him or her;
9. Shows arrogant, haughty behaviors or attitudes.

Histrionic Personality Disorder
A pervasive pattern of excessive emotionality and attention seeking, beginning by early adulthood and present in a variety of contexts, as indicated by five (or more) of the following:
1. Is uncomfortable in situations in which he or she is not the center of attention;
2. Interaction with others is often characterized by inappropriately sexually seductive or provocative behavior;
3. Displays rapidly shifting and shallow expressions of emotion;
4. Consistently uses physical appearance to draw attention to self;
5. Shows self-dramatization, theatricality, and exaggerated expression of emotion;
6. Is suggestible, i.e. easily influenced by others or circumstances;
7. Considers relationships to be more intimate than they actually are.

[14] Janet Johnston and Vivien Roseby, *In the Name of the Child: A Developmental Approach to Understanding and Helping Children of Conflicted and Violent Divorce* (1997) provides a searing, heartbreaking, and highly informative depiction of the world of high-conflict divorce and its impact on children. My copy is filled with blue highlighter, which could just as easily be tears of frustration and sorrow. High conflict divorce is fueled by the truly unspeakable pain residing at the core of the divorcing spouses. Whether it be a result of earlier, childhood, emotional traumas or other overwhelming challenges, the explosive forces unleashed can truly be described as nuclear. Years ago, when I was asked to give my first talk on the

psychology of divorce, colleague and friend, Wendy Hutchins-Cook, PhD, recommended I read this book. I am still indebted for this wise suggestion, despite the troubling nature of the subject matter.

[15] Janet Johnston and Linda Campbell, *Impasses of Divorce: The Dynamics and Resolution of Family Conflict (1999)*. Janet Johnston is, perhaps, the foremost observer of post-divorce challenges and adjustment. Anything she has written will be enlightening to both professional and layperson.

[16] Dan Siegel, *The Mindful Brain: Reflection and Attunement in the Cultivation of Well-Being* (2007). Dan Siegel is a child psychiatrist, writer, educator, and warrior. The guy is indefatigable. His calling over the past number of years has apparently been to explain interpersonal neurobiology (the way our relationships with others in early life impacts brain development and then how the developed brain— however it turns out—impacts our relationships with others). His book *Mindsight*, written in 2010, is the most accessible to the general public on this subject. The man is a wealth of compassion and knowledge. Read him. Listen to him. Learn from him.

[17] Johnston and Campbell, *Impasses of Divorce* (see Note 27).

[18] E. Mavis Hetherington and John Kelly, *For Better or for Worse: Divorced Reconsidered* (2002). Hetherington's work is so important that I spent some time describing it in the text. She and Wallerstein are, perhaps, the two most prolific researchers and writers addressing divorce and its impact on children and the adults impacted. While Wallerstein believed that divorce left a permanent scar on the psyches of the children impacted, Hetherington did not share that view. Her research suggested that children emerge from their parents' divorce healthy and capable of intimate relationships. My experience tends to jibe with Hetherington's conclusions. As I have said countless times, the *one* variable that seems to impact children's management of their parents' divorce is the degree to which they are shielded from parental conflict (thus, the tragedy of the children studied by Johnston and Roseby).

[19] Dr. Susan Gamache is one of the brighter lights of the collaborative community. A therapist, mediator, and trainer from Vancouver, B.C., she has written extensively on divorce and the collaborative process. Given that we in the Seattle area are so close to Vancouver, B.C. (and

Vancouver, WA, for that matter!), we are lucky to have this fantastic resource so close to us.

[20] Isolina Ricci, PhD, *Mom's House, Dad's House – Making Two Homes for Your Child (1997).* Simply put, a venerable classic, which, along with Bonnell and Little's book (see Note 34) has been the go-to guide on co-parenting after divorce.

[21] This excerpt is from the interview with Dan Siegel in the Family Courts Review issue referenced in the text. This volume contains many interviews with stellars in the field.

[22] Karen Bonnell and Kristin Little, *The Co-Parents' Handbook: Raising Well-Adjusted, Resilient and Resourceful Children in a Two-Home Family from Little Ones to Young Adults* (2014). Until this book was published, my go-to recommendation to parents wanting guidance in co-parenting after divorce was Isolina Ricci's classic, *Mom's House, Dad's House.* While still occupying a valued place in my library, it is now a co-recommendation, together with Bonnell and Little's volume. My preference for the latter resides in its relative brevity and abundance of practical and realistic scenarios and advice.

[23] Joan Kelly and Michael Lamb have, together, advocated strongly for consideration of the importance of fathers in the raising of children. Lamb, particularly, has long bemoaned the assumption that mothers are the default primary parental figure for children. His arguments are clear, cogent, and insistent. His voice *needs* to be clear, as he has for years pushed against the tide of the conventional wisdom favoring maternal caregiving. Yet, then again, the conventional wisdom *does* arise in part from research and in part from broad experience.

[24] Robert Baruch Bush and Joseph Folger, *The Promise of Mediation: The Transformative Approach to Conflict* (2004). This book marked a bit of a sea-change in mediators' thinking about the work they do. Prior to that, a prevailing ethic in the field tended to overvalue the mediator's evaluation of the rightness of a particular outcome. Bush and Folger's work was an extension, in the field of mediation, of the increased recognition of client autonomy in the service professions of law and mediation. It is a valuable contribution, both in its content and in the manner in which it extended this particular conversation in the field.

[25] The Uniform Collaborative Law Act (U.C.L.A.) has been passed in a number of states, and more are added each year, as lawyers become more familiar and comfortable with this process. When a legislature

passes this act (it is "uniform" because it is identical in all states) this serves as a strong step toward recognition and legitimacy of the collaborative process in that state.

APPENDIX

BOOKS

Following are a handful of books which will give the divorcing person additional information and advice. These are not, by any stretch, a reflection of all the available books on the subject. They are just the ones that have come across my radar over the years and which I have found extremely helpful.

The Co-Parents' Handbook – Raising Well-Adjusted, Resilient and Resourceful Kids in a Two-Home Family from Little Ones to Young Adults by Karen Bonnell and Kristin Little: For years my go-to book for parents who were ending their relationship was *Mom's House/Dad's House* by Isolina Ricci. It was, and remains, a classic. Yet, when I was introduced to this more compact volume by my Northwest colleagues I made the switch and now recommend Bonnell and Little's book to all my divorcing clients in mediation. The thing I like the most about this book is that they describe so many current and pressing concerns parents have – questions that are so good, but which you might not think to ask. How to think (and talk) about dividing the children's possessions between the homes; what are the rules you will want to talk about and make consistent between the homes; how to talk to the children about a parent's new partner; how do you set up a protocol for communication so that it can be effective and smooth. The book is as practical as you can get and full of examples of dialogues between parents and children to help guide the divorced parent through some of the most difficult patches. "How to" to the max.

Marriage, a History: How Love Conquered Marriage by Stephanie Coontz: Probably the only one in this group that just an outright history book. Oh but what a history book! Nobody gets marriage and its many twists and turn over the last many hundred years as does Stephanie Coontz. Full of fascinating factoids that bring us right up to the present day. When people say, "Marriage has been _____ for millennia, they should read this book. Did you know that inability to consummate a marriage was grounds for divorce in medieval times *and* in order to establish this particular problem, the man had to attempt coitus with "wise women summoned around the bed for many nights." If he was unable to demonstrate an erection, his impotence was established. Coontz tells us that it was not until the Victorian age that marriage for love became a standard and with this change in the basis for marriage, the justification for divorce also changed. Ultimately, the no-fault divorce revolution was a product of this relatively new idea about love and marriage. A fun journey made all the more enjoyable by Coontz' delightful prose.

The Happy Lawyer by Nancy Levit and Douglas Linder: This book is an excellent combination of two very important topics. One is the epidemic of unhappiness among the lawyers in our world. Much of the ideas set forth in the first chapter of this book are mirrored in Levit and Linder's work. They introduce us to the, perhaps strange, notion that lawyers are people – with hopes, dreams, fears and their own relationships. Institutionally, the world of legal practice seems designed to dispirit this group of people who are otherwise interesting and interested...and very full of life. The other part of this book contains a wonderful discussion of a topic that is so important to the challenge of divorce recovery, but is only tangentially addressed here. That is the science of happiness. Martin Seligman developed the field of Positive Psychology from his roost at the University of Pennsylvania and, like EFT and Collaborative Law, it has coursed across the country – attracting adherents by the thousands. This book explores what Seligman learned, and then taught, as it relates to lawyers. The book is an excellent treatment of both topics, which have so much salience to the life and work of lawyers. You know, the ones' who have been trained to help with divorce? You know, Divorce, the subject of this book?

The Collaborative Way to Divorce by Stu Webb and Ron Ouskey: (Webb was discussed in the book. Ouskey was one of the first inspirational leaders of the IACP. An excellent description of the Collaborative Law Process if you need more after reading this book and visiting the web sites suggested here.) This is one of the original discussions of Collaborative Divorce for the layperson and remains a classic in the field.

The Parenting Plan Handbook by Karen Bonnell and Felicia Malsby Soleil: Written as a DYI guide, accompanied by videos and worksheets, this volume walks divorcing parents through all the steps, and all the decisions that you need to make in order to arrive at a satisfying, durable, parenting plan.

The Good Divorce by Constance Ahrons, PhD: Many years ago, when the only way anybody thought about divorcing was for each person to get their own lawyer and duke it out in the trenches, Constance Ahrons wrote a flood of wise and compassionate books and articles cautioning us to stop the madness. There is a better way and nobody wrote about the why and the how of it quite like Ahrons.

COLLABORATIVE LAW COMMUNITIES

To truly appreciate the intensity of the passion that the collaborative law movement has unleashed, one need only gaze at the list of regional organizations that have sprouted up, from coast-to-coast. You will see from any review of a handful of these sites that each provides identification and links to involved professionals. You will also see that some web sites only list attorneys, while others include (as members of the organizations) both mental health and financial professionals. While it is *critical* that attorneys receive intensive training in order to make the collaborative practice "paradigm shift," *and* attorneys are almost always the portal to a collaborative divorce, in my experience these professionals are not the exclusive guides and support. Mental Health Professionals and Financial Experts are equally valuable in a *collaborative* process. It is preferable, then, that these people not only be included in the web sites, but also have a leadership role in the communities. The IACP has maintained this emphasis from its inception.

Parent Organization

International Academy of Collaborative Professionals (IACP):
https://www.collaborativepractice.com

Alaska

Alaska Association of Collaborative Professionals:
http://alaskacollaborative.org

Arizona

Collaborative Divorce Professionals of Arizona:
http://collaborativedivorcearizona.com

Collaborative Law Group of Southern Arizona:
http://www.divorcewisely.comindex.html

Arkansas

Collaborative Family Lawyers of Arkansas, Inc.:
http://collaborativefamilylawyersofarkansas.com

California

Collaborative Practice California: http://cpcal.org

Sacramento Collaborative Practice Group: http://www.divorceoption.com

Collaborative Family Law Group of San Diego:
http://www.collaborativefamilylawsandiego.com

Collaborative Practice San Francisco:
http://www.collaborativepracticesanfrancisco.com

Los Angeles Collaborative Family Law Association: http://www.lacfla.org

San Joaquin Valley Collaborative Divorce:
http://www.sanjoaquincollaborativedivorce.com

Colorado

Collaborative Divorce Professionals of Colorado:
http://www.coloradocollaborativedivorceprofessionals.com

Denver Collaborative Divorce: http://www.denvercollaborativedivorce.net/

Rocky Mountain Collaborative Law Professionals: http://www.rmclp.com

Connecticut

Connecticut Collaborative Divorce Group:
http://www.ctcollaborativedivorce.com

Central Connecticut Collaborative Family Law Group:
http://www.cccflg.com

Collaborative Divorce Lawyers Assoc. of Greater Hartford, Connecticut:
http://www.collaborative-divorce.com

The Collaborative Divorce Team of Connecticut:
http://www.collaborativedivorceteamct.com

Litchfield County Collaborative Divorce Group: http://lccdg.com

Florida

Collaborative Family Law Council of Florida:
http://collaborativecouncilflorida.com

The Collaborative Family Law Group of Central Florida: http://www.cfl-cfl.com

Tampa Bay Collaborative Divorce Group:
http://www.tampabaycollaborative.com

Collaborative Family Law Group of Northeast Florida:
http://www.collaborativecfl.com

Collaborative Family Law Professionals of South Florida:
http://www.collaborativefamilylawfl.com

Georgia

Collaborative Law Institute of Georgia: http://www.divorce-with-benefits.comindex.php

Atlanta Collaborative Divorce Alliance: http://www.atl-divorce.com

Hawaii

Collaborative Divorce Hawaii Practice Group: http://collaborativedivorcehawaii.org

Illinois

Collaborative Law Institute of Illinois: http://collablawil.org

Indiana

Central Indiana Association of Collaborative Professionals: http://collaborative-divorce.org

Iowa

Central Iowa Academy of Collaborative Professionals: http://iowacollaborativedivorce.com

Collaborative Lawyers of Eastern Iowa: http://www.collaborateiowa.org

Northwest Iowa Collaborative Law Professionals: http://www.nwiacollaborate.org

Kansas

Collaborative Divorce Professionals of Greater Kansas City: http://www.collablawmo.com

Collaborative Divorce Kansas City: http://www.collaborativedivorcekansascity.net/

Kentucky

Academy of Collaborative Professionals of Northern Kentucky: http://www.nkcfl.com

Kentucky Collaborative Family Network, Inc.: http://www.kycollaborativedivorce.com

Maryland

Maryland Collaborative Law Association:
http://www.baltimorecollaborativedivorceprofessionals.com

Collaborative Divorce Association, Inc.: http://collaborativedivorcemd.com

Maryland Collaborative Practice Council:
http://www.marylandcollaborativepractice.com

Massachusetts

Massachusetts Collaborative Law Council: http://massclc.org

Michigan

Collaborative Practice Institute of Michigan:
http://www.collaborativepracticemi.org

Collaborative Divorce Professionals of West Michigan:
http://gentlerdivorce.com

Collaborative Divorce Professionals of Southeast Michigan:
http://michigancollaborativedivorce.com

Up North Collaborative Divorce Professionals:
http://www.upnorthcollaborativedivorce.com

Minnesota

Collaborative Law Institute of Minnesota: http://www.collaborativelaw.org

Collaborative Divorce Minnesota: http://collaborativedivorceminnesota.com

Missouri

Collaborative Divorce Professionals of Greater Kansas City:
http://www.collablawmo.com

Collaborative Family Law Association (St. Louis):
http://stlouiscollaborativelaw.com

Nebraska

Nebraska Academy of Collaborative Professionals:
http://collaborativedivorcene.com

Nevada

Nevada County Collaborative Divorce Group:
http://www.nevadacountycollaborative.com

New Hampshire

Collaborative Law Alliance of New Hampshire:
http://collaborativelawnh.org

New Jersey

New Jersey Collaborative Law Group:
http://newjerseycollaborativelawgroup.com

Collaborative Divorce Professionals: http://njcollaborativeprofessionals.com

New Jersey Council of Collaborative Law Groups:
http://www.collaboratenj.org

Jersey Shore Collaborative Law Group: http://jsclg.org

South Jersey Collaborative Law Group:
http://southjerseycollaborativelawgroup.com

New Mexico

New Mexico Collaborative Practice Group:
http://nmcollaborativedivorce.org

Albuquerque Collaborative Divorce Alternatives:
http://www.albuquerquecollaborativedivorcealternatives.com

New York

New York Association of Collaborative Professionals:
http://www.nycollaborativeprofessionals.org

New York Unified Courts – Collaborative Divorce Center:
http://www.nycourts.gov/ip/collablaw/

Hudson Valley Collaborative Divorce Association:
http://www.collabdivorce-ny.com

Central New York Collaborative Family Law Professionals:
http://cnycollaborativepractice.com

North Carolina

Collaborative Divorce Professionals (Raleigh, Durham, Chapel Hill):
http://www.collaborativedivorceexperts.com

Triad Collaborative Family Law Practice Group:
http://triadcollaborative.com

North Dakota

North Dakota Collaborative Law Group: http://www.nddivorce.com

Ohio

Cleveland Academy of Collaborative Professionals:
http://www.collaborativepracticecleveland.com

Central Ohio Academy of Collaborative Divorce Professionals:
http://www.winwindivorce.org

Cincinnati Academy of Collaborative Professionals:
http://www.collaborativelaw.com

Northeast Ohio Collaborative Professionals: http://abetterwaytodivorce.org

Oklahoma

Oklahoma Academy of Collaborative Professionals:
http://www.yourdivorcechoice.com

Oregon

Oregon Association of Collaborative Professionals:
http://www.collaborativepracticeoregon.org

Pennsylvania

Collaborative Professionals of Central Pennsylvania:
http://www.collaborativelawpa.com

Collaborative Law Association of Southwestern Pennsylvania:
http://www.clasplaw.org

Collaborative Law Professionals of Southeast Pennsylvania:
http://gocollaborativepa.com

South Carolina

South Carolina Collaborative Law Institute: http://www.sccli.org

Tennessee

Middle Tennessee Collaborative Alliance: http://www.mtcollab.com

Memphis Collaborative Alliance:
http://memphiscollaborativealliance.comindex.html

Texas

The Collaborative Institute of Texas: http://www.collablawtexas.com

Dallas Alliance of Collaborative Family Lawyers:
http://www.dallascollaborativelaw.com

Utah

Association of Collaborative Professionals of Utah: http://www.utahacp.org

Vermont

Central Vermont Collaborative Law Practice Group:
http://www.centralvermontcollaborativelaw.com

Virginia

Collaborative Professionals of Northern Virginia: http://www.cpnova.com

Virginia Collaborative Professionals:
https://www.vacollaborativepractice.com

Washington

Collaborative Professionals of Washington:
http://www.collaborativeprofessionalsofwashington.org

King County Collaborative Law: http://kingcountycollab.org

Whatcom Collaborative Law Professionals:
http://whatcomcollaborativelaw.com

Kitsap Collaborative Law Professionals: http://collaborativekitsap.org

Wisconsin

Collaborative Family Law Council of Wisconsin:
http://www.collabdivorce.com

ARIZONA COLLABORATIVE LAW WEB SITE

Is Collaborative Law Right For You?

Quick Yes/No Quiz

1.   Do you and your spouse have trouble communicating about your divorce?

2.   Do emotions sometimes stop you from expressing your opinions?

3.   Would you like to know how your spouse feels about your separation?

4.   Would you like help learning how to reach agreements with your spouse?

5.   Would you like to divide your property in an way that you can live with?

6.   Has one spouse been in control of your finances during the marriage?

7.   Would you like help knowing how you are going to pay for the divorce?

8.   Would you like a better understanding of your current financial picture?

9.   Would you like to know how your divorce will affect your financial future?

10. Would you like to develop a financial plan that you can live with?

11. Do you have children?

12. Would you like to know age appropriate ways to discuss divorce with children?

13. Do you know your children's feelings about your separation?

14. Would you like your children's opinions to be considered in

your divorce?

15. Would you like to reach agreements about the children that you can live with?

16. Would you like help understanding the legal steps involved in a divorce?

17. Do you know your legal rights before, during or after the divorce?

18. Would you like legal representation during your divorce?

19. Would you like help completing the divorce paperwork?

20. Would you like to know ways to modify agreements in the future if necessary?

If you answered YES to 10 or more questions, collaborative divorce may be for you. Contact a collaborative professional for more information.

COLLABORATIVE PROCESS
PARTICIPATION AGREEMENT

Ozzie Nelson and Harriet Nelson ("the Parties") have chosen to use the Collaborative Process to resolve, without intervention from a court or other tribunal, all issues arising from the dissolution of their marriage. They have selected Carl Collaborator and Nina Nonadversarial (collectively "the Lawyers" and individually "Lawyer") to assist them. The terms of the Washington Uniform Collaborative Law Act, RCW 7.77, et seq., ("UCLA") apply to this Collaborative Process.

1.   Principles

We agree that these principles form the foundation of our Collaborative Process:

> Acting with honesty, transparency, and candor;
> Demonstrating cooperation, respect, integrity and dignity;
> Identifying and addressing the interests and needs of all;
> Focusing on the future well-being of ourselves and our children;
> Committing to resolve matters directly and without court intervention.

We are each voluntarily choosing the Collaborative process and the responsibilities that these principles entail.

2.   Communication

The Parties commit to communicate effectively with each other in a respectful and constructive manner, and to explore and express their interests, goals, desires, and options without criticism from the other. The Parties and Lawyers shall uphold a high standard of integrity, and shall abide by the attached "Rules of Good Faith in the Collaborative Process" which are part of this agreement.

The Parties authorize the Lawyers to communicate directly with either Party, including the Party who is not their own client.

3.   Children's Issues

Ozzie and Harriet agree to make every effort to keep their children's best interests in the forefront when discussing children's issues. They acknowledge that the Parties' disputes are inappropriate to share with and can be harmful to their children, and therefore will not be discussed with or in the presence of their children.

4.   Disclosure of Information

The Parties each agree to promptly provide all information that is reasonably material for resolution, including full disclosure of all assets, income, expectancies, debts, budgeting and other information, whether or not such information has been requested. Additionally, the Parties will supplement and/or update information as necessary to ensure its continued accuracy.

Because both Parties are expected to provide complete and accurate information, the final settlement documents will include sworn statements that the Parties have fully and fairly disclosed all material information.

5.   Integrity

No Party or Lawyer may knowingly withhold or misrepresent information material to the Collaborative process or otherwise act or fail to act in a way that knowingly undermines or takes unfair advantage of the Collaborative process. If a Party knowingly withholds or misrepresents information material to the Collaborative process, or otherwise acts in a way that undermines or takes unfair advantage of the Collaborative process, and continues after being advised of his or her obligations, this will mandate the termination of the Collaborative process.

6.   Professional Team Members, Consultants, and Experts

Except for the lawyers, all professional team members, experts, and consultants will be jointly hired and work for both Parties. Unless there is specific agreement otherwise, neither party will have experts or consultants who are not jointly hired.

All professional team members are independent from one another, have no financial connections, fee-setting, fee-sharing, or referral fee arrangements with one another. The professional team members are not agents for each other.

Professional fees may be incurred in professional team conferences, including conferences that may occur before the Parties have met with or formally retained the other team professionals. The parties agree to pay the fees of all professionals incurred in professional team conferences, including those professionals who are expected to be hired but may not yet have met with the parties.

The fees of the parties' lawyers are likely not identical. The Parties understand that no Collaborative professional can continue to provide services without being paid. For that reason, the Parties undertake to keep payment of all professional fees current. Any disagreements between the parties about ultimate responsibility for payment of such fees will be resolved when other financial issues are resolved.

Mental health professionals who serve on the professional team as coaches or child specialists are retained for discrete Collaborative Process purposes, and do not provide diagnosis or treatment of mental conditions.

7.   Beginning and End of the Collaborative Process

The Parties agree that the Collaborative Process begins when they sign this Participation Agreement and ends (a) upon reaching resolution in a signed writing, or (b) upon termination of the Collaborative Process. The beginning and end of the Collaborative Process does not define the relationship between parties and professionals.

8.   No Court or Adversarial Intervention

During the Collaborative Process neither Party shall take any court action (including but not limited to contested proceedings such as motions, restraining orders, trial, etc., and other procedures of the court system) or utilize any other adversarial process other than that which is mutually agreed, mandated by an applicable court rule or court order, or necessitated by a bona fide emergency. No formal "discovery" procedures (court-rule based information gathering) will be used unless specifically agreed by the Parties.

9.   Lawyer Disqualification

Each party has retained their Lawyer for a limited purpose, which is solely to provide services within the Collaborative Process. The Parties agree that a lawyer who represented a party under this Collaborative Process, and any lawyer in a law firm with which such a lawyer is associated, shall be disqualified from representing a party in a court or other adversarial proceeding related to the matter under this Collaborative Process.

However, a party's lawyer under the Collaborative Process may represent a party to request a tribunal to approve an agreement resulting from the Collaborative Process, or to seek or defend an emergency order to protect the health, safety, welfare, or interest of a party if a successor lawyer is not immediately available to represent that party. As soon as that party is represented by a successor lawyer, or when reasonable measures have been taken to address the imminent emergency, the disqualification provision above shall apply.

10. Termination of the Collaborative Process

The Parties agree that their participation in the Collaborative Process is voluntary and that any party has the right to terminate the process at any time. Termination occurs if:

(a) A Party gives notice to the other parties and lawyers that the process has ended; or

(b) A Party begins a judicial or other adjudicative procedure without the agreement of all parties; or

(c) A Party discharges a Lawyer or the Lawyer withdraws from further representation of the party. However, in such event, the Collaborative Process may continue provided that within thirty (30) days, the unrepresented Party engages a successor collaborative lawyer and the Parties consent in writing to continue the Collaborative Process.

If a Party terminates the Collaborative Law Process, the Parties agree to attend one more joint session within thirty days of giving notice, unless waived by agreement or failure to schedule the joint session within the thirty day period.

If a Lawyer withdraws or terminates the Collaborative process, that Lawyer will notify the other professionals in the case.

11. Waiting Period If Process Terminates

Absent a bona fide emergency, there will be a thirty day waiting period prior to any court hearing or other proceeding (such as a deposition) if the Collaborative Process terminates. The waiting period allows each Party to retain a new lawyer and make an orderly transition without undue surprise. Either Party may bring this provision to the attention of the Court to request a postponement of a hearing or proceeding.

If the Collaborative Process terminates, the provisions of Section 13, "Temporary Rights and Obligations," shall remain in effect until changed by mutual agreement or court order.

12. Confidentiality and Privilege

All Collaborative Law communications between and among Parties and professional team members, and all work product generated by professionals during the Collaborative Process, are confidential and shall remain confidential as to those not directly involved in the matter subject to the Collaborative Process.

The parties understand that mental health professionals have certain mandatory reporting requirements established by law. Lawyers have more restrictive mandatory reporting requirements established by law. The above confidentiality provision does not apply to communications initiated by a lawyer or other professional that are required or authorized to be made by law, such as reporting abuse or actual or threatened criminal activity.

The parties recognize that the UCLA provides for certain privileges in an adjudicative proceeding. The parties agree that the opinions and work product of experts and consultants in the Collaborative Process shall be considered Collaborative law communications subject to the privilege in the UCLA. Additionally, in any court, arbitration, or other legal proceeding between the Parties, neither will offer evidence of any information created for use in the Collaborative Process, except for: (1) signed agreements, (2) documents that are signed under penalty of perjury, and (3) as agreed between the client and professional under the terms of this section 12.

13. Temporary Rights and Obligations

Unless agreed otherwise in writing (which may include email):

A.   The Parties will maintain the residential arrangements of the children;

B.   Major assets may be transferred only by agreement;

C.   Major expenses (anything above normal expenses), will be incurred only by agreement;

D.   All insurance coverage will be maintained and continued without change in coverage or beneficiary designation; and

E.   Any changes to utilities, accounts of any kind, or credit card accounts will be only by agreement.

14. Lawyer's Commitment

The Parties understand that each Lawyer has a professional duty to represent solely his or her own client, and is not the lawyer for the other Party. The other Party is not a third party beneficiary of a Lawyer's work for his/her own client.

15. Enforceability of Agreements

Signed agreements reached in the Collaborative Process are intended to be enforceable and therefore may be presented to the court as a basis for an order, which may be retroactive to the date of the agreement. **Unsigned agreements are not intended to be enforceable absent agreement of the Parties**.

Parties:

Dated: _____   Dated: _____

_____   _____
Ozzie Nelson, Husband   Harriet Nelson, Wife

Collaborative Lawyers:

In signing below, each of us affirms our intent to represent our clients in the manner agreed between them above, to proceed in a manner consistent with the letter and spirit of this document, and to abide by all applicable protocols of King County Collaborative Law and the Ethical Standards for Collaborative Professionals of the International Academy of Collaborative Professionals.

_____   _____
Carl Collaborative   Nina Nonadversarial
Attorney for Wife   Attorney for Husband

Other Collaborative Team Professionals:

In signing below, each of us affirms our intent to proceed in a manner consistent with the letter and spirit of this document, and to abide by all applicable protocols of King County Collaborative Law and the Ethical Standards for Collaborative Professionals of the International Academy of Collaborative Professionals.

_____
Collaborative Divorce Coach

_____
Collaborative Financial Specialist

_____
Collaborative Child Specialist

Rules of Good Faith in the Collaborative Process

Please place your initials at the bottom of this page indicating you agree and understand. We encourage questions about these rules.

1.   We agree to proceed in "Good Faith." Good faith means to abide by the rules of common courtesy, keep an open mind, be willing to explore options without holding a fixed position, and share all pertinent information.

2.   At all times, in meetings and in-between meetings, we will endeavor to treat each other and our children with respect.

3.   We will honor the other's privacy, including belongings and living space.

4.   We agree to convert complaints into neutral requests to the best of our abilities, and to refrain from blaming and negative assumptions based on the past behavior of our partner.

5.   We agree to work productively in the "here and now" keeping everyone's future well-being in mind.

6.   We agree to share our most important priorities, goals, and concerns, so that they can be considered and addressed. We agree to take the priorities, goals, and concerns of our partner into account.

7.   In communications outside of joint sessions, we agree to communicate respectfully, and to honor any requests to defer a discussion to a later time.

8.   We agree not to threaten to withdraw from the Collaborative Process or to go to court as a means of achieving a desired outcome or forcing a settlement.

9.   We agree not to take advantage of inconsistencies, miscalculations, wrong assumptions or omissions of the other. Instead, we shall disclose them and seek to have them corrected at the earliest opportunity, and shall instruct our lawyers and the other professionals to do the same.

10.   We agree to immediately voice to our own Lawyer any concerns or questions about the Collaborative Process.

11.   We agree to not destroy any documents or data that could be relevant or important to the other.

_____

_____

About the Author

Joseph Shaub has been an *attorney* for more than forty years and *marriage and family therapist* for more than twenty. Since arriving in Seattle from Southern California in 1995, he has been a popular columnist for both lawyer and therapist publications in the Pacific Northwest and is a sought-after speaker. His many workshops, including *Family Law for the Mental Health Professional; The Psychology of Divorce; Confidentiality, Privilege and Recordkeeping for Therapists;* and *Basic* and *Advanced Training in Collaborative Law* have been mainstays in the Northwest Community. Joe and his wife can either be found hiking local trails or reading by the fireside, depending on the season. Their daughter is pursuing a graduate degree in nutrition policy and they eat frequently to test her theories.

All inquiries and comments are welcome.
Contact joe@josephshaub.com.

You are invited to visit Joe's website: www.josephshaub.com.

Made in the USA
San Bernardino, CA
19 April 2018